Tafsīr al-Qurṭubī

Introduction

Tafsīr al-Qurṭubī

The General Judgments of the Qur'an and Clarification of what it contains of the Sunnah and *Āyahs* of Discrimination

Abū 'Abdullāh Muḥammad ibn Aḥmad ibn Abī Bakr ibn Farḥ al-Anṣārī al-Khazrajī al-Andalusī al-Qurṭubī

INTRODUCTION

translated by
Aisha Bewley

Diwan Press
Classical and Contemporary Books on Islam and Sufism

Published by: Diwan Press Ltd.

Website: www.diwanpress.com
E-mail: info@diwanpress.com

By: Abu Muhammad ibn Ahmad al-Qurtubi
Translated by: Aisha Abdarrahman Bewley
Edited by: Abdalhaqq Bewley

A catalogue record of this book is available from the British Library.

ISBN13: 978-1-908892-57-7 (Paperback)
978-1-908892-56-0 (Hardback)
978-1-908892-58-4 (Casebound)
978-1-908892-70-6 (ePub & Kindle)

Printed by: Lightning Source

Contents

Table of Transliterations vii

Translator's note viii

The general virtues of the Qur'an and encouragement to study it. The excellence of the one who seeks it, recites it, listens to it and acts by it. 6

How to recite the Book of Allah and what is disliked and forbidden in respect of it, and people's disagreement about that 11

Cautioning the people of the Qur'an and scholars against showing off 17

What someone who knows the Qur'an must do and not neglect to do 20

The syntax of the Qur'an, learning it and studying it, and the reward for the one who recites the Qur'an with proper inflections 23

What is reported about the excellence of *tafsīr* of the Qur'an and those who do it 26

What is reported about the one who is a bearer of the Qur'an, who he is and those who are hostile to him 27

The respect and esteem for the Qur'an which is mandatory for someone who recites and bears the Qur'an 27

What is reported regarding threats against engaging in *tafsīr* of the Qur'an by means of opinion (*ra'y*) or being bold in doing that, and the ranks of the commentators 32

The Book being explained by the Sunnah, and what has been transmitted about that 37

How to learn and understand the Book of Allah and the Sunnah of His Prophet ﷺ, and what has been narrated about it being easier for someone who used to act by it without memorising it 40

The meaning of the words of the Prophet ﷺ, "The Qur'an was revealed in seven *aḥruf* (dialects/modes)." 42

Section on the seven readings 46

Section: The hadith of 'Umar and Hishām 47

The collection of the Qur'an and the reason 'Uthmān had copies of the Qur'an copied out and burned the rest. The memorisation of the Qur'an by the Companions in the time of the Prophet ﷺ 49

Section 54

Section 55

What has come about the order of the *sūrah*s and *āyah*s of the Qur'an, its vowelling and dots, its *ḥizb*s and tens, the number of its letters, *juz'*s, words and *āyah*s 58

Section 61

Section 61

Section 62

Section 62

The meaning of the words *sūrah, āyah, kalimah* (word) and *ḥarf* (letter) 63

Does the Qur'an contain words which are not Arabic? 65

Points about the inimitability of the Qur'an, preconditions of the miracle and its reality 66

Section 68

Information about hadiths forged about the excellence of the *sūrah*s of the Qur'an and other matters 73

What has come on the refutation of those who attack the Qur'an and oppose the text of 'Uthmān by adding to it or removing some of it 75

Seeking Refuge with Allah from Shayṭān 78

The *Basmalah* 81

Table of Transliterations

ء	’	ض	ḍ
ا	a	ط	ṭ
ب	b	ظ	ẓ
ت	t	ع	‘
ث	th	غ	gh
ج	j	ف	f
ح	ḥ	ق	q
خ	kh	ك	k
د	d	ل	l
ذ	dh	م	m
ر	r	ن	n
ز	z	ه	h
س	s	و	w
ش	sh	ي	y
ص	ṣ		

Long vowel		Short vowel	
ا	ā	ـَ	a [*fatḥah*]
و	ū	ـُ	u [*ḍammah*]
ي	ī	ـِ	i [*kasrah*]
أَوْ	aw		
أَيْ	ay		

Translator's note

There are minor omissions in the text. Some poems have been omitted which the author quotes to illustrate a point of grammatical usage or as an example of orthography or the usage of a word, often a derivative of the root of the word used in the *āyah*, but not the actual word used. Often it is difficult to convey the sense in English. Occasionally the author explores a grammatical matter or a tangential issue, and some of these may have been shortened. English grammatical terms used to translate Arabic grammatical terms do not have the exact same meaning, sometimes rendering an exact translation of them problematic and often obscure.

The end of a *juz'* may vary by an *āyah* or two in order to preserve relevant passages.

بسم الله الرحمن الرحيم

Introduction

In the Name of Allah, the All-Merciful, Most Merciful

We seek His help and may Allah bless our master Muḥammad and his family and Companions and grant them abundant peace. Thus speaks the *faqīh*, imam of knowledge and action, the hadith scholar, Abū 'Abdullāh Muḥammad ibn Aḥmad ibn Abī Bakr ibn Farḥ al-Anṣārī al-Khazrajī al-Andalusī, then al-Qurṭubī:

Praise belongs to Allah who began by praising Himself before any praiser praised Him! I testify that there is no god but Allah alone with no partner, the Lord who is One and Self-Sustaining, the Living, Self-Subsistent Who does not die, the Master of Majesty and Nobility and immense gifts, He Who has spoken the Qur'an, He Who created the human being and blessed him with faith and sent His Messenger Muḥammad ﷺ to make the message clear. He sent him with the Clear Book, which distinguishes between doubt and certainty, which eloquent men cannot oppose and intelligent men cannot contradict. They cannot produce its like, even if they help one another. He made its examples lessons for those who reflect on them and His commands guidance for those who study them. In it He explains the obligatory judgments and differentiates between the lawful and unlawful. In it He repeats admonitions and stories for understanding and different types of metaphors and reports about matters of the Unseen.

Allah Almighty says, '*We have not omitted anything from the Book.*' (6:38) He addresses it to His friends and they understand; and He explains to them what He means in it and they grasp it. So those who recite the Qur'an bear a concealed secret of Allah and guard His preserved knowledge. They are the caliphs of His Prophets and His trustees, who are His people, elite and chosen ones. The Messenger of Allah ﷺ said, 'Allah has his own people (*ahlīn*) among us.' They asked, 'Who are they, Messenger of Allah?' He replied, 'They are the people of the Qur'an, the people of Allah and His élite.' Ibn Mājah transmitted it in the *Sunan* and Abū Bakr al-Bazzār in his *Musnad.*

Anyone who knows the Book of Allah and remembers what has been explained to him in it should be restrained by its prohibitions and fear Allah, be mindful of Him and be ashamed before Him. He has taken on the heavy responsibility of the Messengers and has become a witness at the Rising against any opponents among the people of other religions. Allah Almighty said, '*In this way We have made you a middlemost community, so that you may act as witnesses against mankind.*' (2:143) The proof is against the one who knows it and neglects it, rather than against the one who is lacking in it and ignorant of it. If someone is given knowledge of the Qur'an and does not benefit from it, is not constrained by its prohibitions and is not deterred by it, and commits ugly sins and vile crimes, the Qur'an is an argument against him. The Messenger of Allah ﷺ said, 'The Qur'an is an argument either for you or against you.' Muslim transmitted it. Therefore it is obligatory for anyone chosen by Allah to memorise His Book to have proper respect for it, reflect on the truth of its words, understand its marvels and clarify what is unusual in it. The Almighty says: '*It is a Book We have sent down to you, full of blessings, so let people of intelligence ponder its Signs*' (38:29) and '*Will they not then ponder the Qur'an or are there locks upon their hearts?*' (47:24) May Allah make us among those who respect it properly, reflect on it deeply, implement its justice, fulfil its conditions and do not seek guidance elsewhere! May He guide us to its outward signs and radiant definitive judgments and by it combine for us the best of this world and the Next! He is worthy to be feared and entitled to forgive!

Then He gave to His Messenger clarification of what was unspecified, explanation of what was difficult, and determination of what was probable, so that, as well as conveying the Message, he ﷺ showed his special competence regarding the Revelation which was entrusted to him. Allah says: '*And We have sent down the Reminder to you so that you can make clear to mankind what has been sent down to them.*' (16:44) Then, after the Messenger of Allah ﷺ the scholars were appointed to educe the meanings which it indicates and to point out its principles in order that through *ijtihād* they may reach the knowledge of what is meant. By that they are distinguished from others and are singled out for reward on account of their efforts. Allah Almighty says: '*Allah will raise in rank those of you who believe and those who have been given knowledge.'* (58:11) So the Book became the basis, the Sunnah its clarification, and the deduction of the scholars its exposition and elucidation. Praise be to Allah who has made our breasts the vessels of His Book, our ears the springs of the Sunnah of His Prophet ﷺ, and our aspirations directed to learning the Qur'an and investigating its meanings and unusual words, and through that our seeking to please the Lord of the worlds and rise to knowledge of the *dīn*.

The Book of Allah is the source of all the sciences of the Sharī'ah which convey the Sunnah and the obligatory. It was brought down by the Trustworthy One of heaven to the Trustworthy One of the earth. I thought that I should devote myself to it for my entire life and devote my strength to that cause by writing a brief commentary on it containing some points of *tafsīr*, linguistics, grammar, and recitation, refutation of the people of deviation and misguidance, as well as several hadiths which attest to what we mention in it regarding judgments and the revelation of *āyahs*, thereby combining the meanings of both and explaining what is abstruse in them using the statements of the Salaf and those who followed them. I have done this to remind myself and as a security for the day when I am buried, and as a righteous action to continue beyond my death. Allah says: *'On that Day man will be told what he did and failed to do'* (75:13) and *'Each self will know what it has sent ahead and left behind.'* (82:15) The Prophet ﷺ said, 'When a man dies, his actions are cut off except for three — an ongoing *ṣadaqah* and knowledge which brought benefit and a virtuous child who makes supplication for him.'

I intend in this book to attribute statements to their speakers and hadiths to their compilers. It is said that part of the blessing of knowledge is to ascribe a statement to its speaker. Many unattributed hadiths are reported in books of *tafsīr* and *fiqh* and so the one who reads them does not know who transmitted them. Therefore someone without information about that remains confused and does not know the sound from the weak. It is a vast science. Therefore he does not accept it as evidence until he knows the person to whom it is ascribed among the famous imams and reliable scholars of Islam. We have indicated some of that in this book. Allah is the One Who grants success. I have only used those stories of commentators and reports of historians that are necessary for clarification purposes and also help to elucidate the *āyahs* which contain legal rulings so as to disclose the full meaning and guide one to what is demanded by them. With every *āyah* I have included whatever rulings it contains and other matters that we will explain, when it contains reasons for its revelation, unusual commentary and wisdoms. If it does not contain any legal judgement, I talk about its interpretation.

The full title of this book is: The General Judgments of the Qur'an and Clarification of what it contains of the Sunnah and *āyah*s of Discrimination. May Allah make it sincerely for His sake and grant me and my parents the benefit of it. He hears the supplication and is quick to respond. Amen.

The general virtues of the Qur'an and encouragement to study it. The excellence of the one who seeks it, recites it, listens to it and acts by it.

This topic is vast and scholars have written many books about it. We will mention some points that point out the excellence of the Qur'an and what Allah has prepared for its people when they are sincere for His sake and act by it. The first aspect of the excellence of the Qur'an that the believer should be aware of is that it is from the Lord of the worlds and is uncreated. It consists of unparalleled words and has a quality which has no equivalent or like. It comes from the Light of Allah's Essence. Recitation of it is by the voices of the reciters and their vocalisation. It is their acquisition and they are commanded to do it as an obligation in certain acts of worship and it is recommended at many times. They are reproved if they avoid it, and are rewarded for doing it and punished for abandoning it. This is something that the Muslims, the people of the Truth, agree on. Traditions state that and well-known reports prove it.

Reward and punishment are only connected to what is part of what people earn, as will be explained. Were it not that Allah had placed in the hearts of His slaves the strength to bear it so that they can reflect on it, study it and remember what it contains regarding obedience to Him, worship and performing their duties and obligations, they would be too weak and would collapse under its weight or perish. How could they bear it when Allah says, '*Had We sent down this Qur'an onto a mountain, you would have seen it humbled, crushed to pieces out of fear of Allah*' (59:21)? What is the strength of hearts compared to that of the mountains? But Allah provided His slaves with the strength to bear what He wishes as a favour and mercy from Him.

As for traditions about this topic, the first is what at-Tirmidhī transmitted from Abū Sa'īd that the Messenger of Allah ﷺ said, 'The blessed and exalted Lord said, "If anyone is distracted from asking Me by the Qur'an and remembrance of Me, I will give him better than what I give to those who ask."' He also said, 'The excellence of the words of Allah over all other words is like the excellence of Allah over His creation.' He said that it is a *ḥasan gharīb* hadith. Abū Muḥammad ad-Dārimī as-Samarqandī reported in his *Musnad* that 'Abdullāh said, 'The seven long *sūrahs* are like the Torah. The *sūrahs* with a hundred *āyahs* are like the Gospel, and the Mathānī is like the Zabūr. The rest of the Qur'an is excellent in itself.'

In at-Tirmidhī, al-Ḥārith reported that 'Alī said, 'I heard the Messenger of Allah ﷺ say, "There will be trials like patches of dark night." I asked, "Messenger of Allah, how can one escape them?" He replied, "The Book of Allah, blessed and exalted be He, contains your history, information about what came before you, news about what will come after you and correct judgment between you. It is decisive, not a jest. Allah will crush any tyrant who abandons it and Allah will misguide whoever seeks guidance from other than it. It is the Firm Rope of Allah, His Clear Light and the Wise Reminder. It is the Straight Path. Passions are not misguided by it, tongues do not become sated with it, and the godfearing do not become bored by it. It does not wear out when it is recited a lot, and its wonders do not cease. It is that which the jinn did not leave once they had heard it. They said, '*We heard a wonderful Qur'an which guides to right guidance.*' (72:1-2) Whoever knows it has knowledge which takes precedence. Whoever utters it speaks the truth. Whoever judges by it is just. Whoever acts by it is rewarded. Whoever calls to it is guided to a straight path. Take it, O one-eyed."' ('One-eyed' referred to al-Ḥārith). Ash-Sha'bī accused al-Ḥārith of lying and of being of no consequence. There are no evident lies from al-Ḥārith, but he is reproved for his excessive love for 'Alī and preferring him to anyone else. Allah knows best, but this is why ash-Sha'bī called him a liar, since he preferred Abū Bakr and states that he was the first to become Muslim. Abū 'Umar ibn 'Abd al-Barr said, 'I think that ash-Sha'bī was punished for what he said about al-Ḥārith al-Hamdānī being a liar.'

Abū Bakr Muḥammad ibn Bashshār ibn Muḥammad al-Anbārī, the linguist and grammarian, says in his book, *The Refutation of the One who Opposes the Recension of 'Uthman*, transmitting from 'Abdullāh ibn Mas'ūd that the Messenger of Allah ﷺ said, 'This Qur'an is the Banquet of Allah. Learn as much as you can from His Banquet. This Qur'an is the Rope of Allah, and it is the Clear Light and Useful Healing. It is a protection for the one who clings to it and a rescue for the one who follows it. It is not crooked and so puts things straight. It does not stray so as to be blamed. Its wonders do not cease. It does not wear out with much repetition. So recite it. Allah will reward you with ten good deeds for every letter of its recitation. I do not say that *Alif-Lām-Mīm* is a letter. Let me not find any of you placing his foot on the other abandoning the recitation of Sūrat al-Baqarah. Shayṭān flees from a house in which Sūrat al-Baqarah is recited. The house most devoid of good is a house empty of the Book of Allah.'

In his *Gharīb* Abū 'Ubayd quotes 'Abdullāh (ibn Mas'ūd): 'This Qur'an is the Banquet of Allah. Whoever enters it is safe.' He said, 'The interpretation of the hadith is that it is a metaphor. The Qur'an is likened to something Allah has prepared for people. They have good and benefit from it. Then He invites them to it.' If the word is *'ma'dubah'*, then it is something that someone prepares and then invites people to partake of. If it is read as *'ma'dabah'*, it means the means of instruction which leads to someone having good manners (*adab*). The evidence for this is found in another hadith: 'This Qur'an is the means of instruction of Allah Almighty, so learn from His means of instruction.' Al-Aḥmar said that both words are from different dialects and mean the same thing, but I have not heard anyone besides him say this. I prefer the first explanation.

Al-Bukhārī transmits from 'Uthmān ibn 'Affān that the Prophet ﷺ said, 'The best of you is the one who learns the Qur'an and teaches it.' Muslim transmitted from Abū Mūsā that the Messenger of Allah ﷺ said, 'The metaphor of a believer who recites the Qur'an is that of a citron – its scent is fragrant and its taste is good. The metaphor of a believer who does not recite the Qur'an is that of a date – it has no scent but its taste is sweet. The metaphor of a hypocrite who recites the Qur'an is that of basil – its scent is fragrant but its taste is bitter. The metaphor of a hypocrite who does not recite the Qur'an is that of colocynth – it has no scent and its taste is bitter.' One variant has 'deviant' instead of 'hypocrite'.

Abū Bakr al-Anbārī mentioned that Aḥmad ibn Yaḥyā al-Ḥulwānī reported from Yaḥyā ibn 'Abd al-Ḥamīd from Hushaym, and from Idrīs from Khalaf from Hushaym from al-'Awwām ibn Ḥawshab that when someone finished the Qur'an, Abū 'Abd ar-Raḥmān as-Sulamī would have him sit before him and put his hand on his head and say to him, 'You! Fear Allah! I do not know of anyone better than you if you act by what you know.' Ad-Dārimī reported that Wahb adh-Dhimārī said, 'If Allah gives someone the Qur'an and he stands reciting it at the ends of the night and the ends of the day and acts by what is in it and dies in obedience, on the Day of Rising Allah will raise him up with the angels and Prophets.'

Muslim related that 'Ā'ishah reported that the Messenger of Allah ﷺ said, 'Someone who recites the Qur'an and is fluent in it is with the noble pious angels. Someone who recites the Qur'an and stammers in it has two rewards, as it is difficult for him.' He will have one reward for the recitation and one reward for the difficulty. The levels of the fluent reciter are all above that, because the Qur'an was difficult for him and then he rose beyond that to be like the angels. Allah knows best.

At-Tirmidhī reports from 'Abdullāh ibn Mas'ūd that the Messenger of Allah ﷺ said, 'Whoever recites a letter of the Book of Allah earns a good deed, and each good deed is worth ten like it. I do not say that *'Alif-Lām-Mīm'* is one letter, but that *alif* is a letter, *lām* is a letter, and *mīm* is a letter.' He said that it is a sound *ḥasan gharīb* hadith by this path of transmission. It is also related *mawqūf*.

Muslim reported that 'Uqbah ibn 'Āmir said, 'The Messenger of Allah ﷺ came out to us while we were in the Ṣuffah and asked, "Which of you would like to go every day to Buṭḥān or to al-'Aqīq and bring two large-humped she-camels from it without wrongdoing?" We said, "Messenger of Allah, all of us would like that!" He said, "Does not one of you go to the mosque and learn or recite two *āyahs* from the Book of Allah? That is better for him than two camels, and three *āyahs* are better for him than three camels, four *āyahs* are better than four camels, and so on regarding the number of camels."'

Abū Hurayrah reported that the Messenger of Allah ﷺ said, 'Allah will relieve anyone who relieves a believer of one of the afflictions of this world of one of the afflictions of the Day of Rising. Allah will give ease in this world and the Next to anyone who eases the hardship of another. Allah will veil anyone who veils another Muslim in this world and the Next. Allah will help His slave as long as His slave is helping his brother. Whoever travels a path on which he seeks knowledge, Allah will make the path to the Garden easy for him. People do not meet in one of the houses of Allah to recite the Book of Allah and study it together without tranquillity descending on them, mercy covering them, angels encircling them and Allah mentioning them to those who are with Him.'

Abū Dāwūd, an-Nasā'ī, ad-Dārimī, and at-Tirmidhī reported that 'Uqbah ibn 'Āmir heard the Prophet ﷺ say, 'The one who recites the Qur'an publicly is like the person who gives his *ṣadaqah* publicly. The one who recites the Qur'an secretly is like the person who conceals his *ṣadaqah*.' At-Tirmidhī said that it is a *ḥasan gharīb* hadith. At-Tirmidhī reported from Abū Hurayrah that the Prophet ﷺ said, 'The Qur'an will come on the Day of Rising and say, "O Lord, robe him!" and He will put on him the crown of nobility. It will say, "O Lord, more!" and He will put on him the robe of honour. Then it will say, "O Lord, be pleased with him!" and He will be pleased with him. It will be said, "Recite and ascend," and he will be increased with a good deed for every *āyah*.' He said that it is a sound hadith.

Abū Dāwūd reported from 'Abdullāh ibn 'Amr that the Messenger of Allah ﷺ said, 'Those who know the Qur'an will be told, "Recite and ascend. Recite slowly as you did in the world below. Your station will be at the last verse you recite."' Ibn Mājah transmits it in the *Sunan* from Abū Sa'īd al-Khudrī who reported that the Messenger of Allah ﷺ said, 'The one who knows the Qur'an will be told, "Recite and ascend." He will recite and rise a degree by every *āyah* until he reaches the last one he has.'

Abū Bakr al-Anbārī transmitted from Abū Umāmah al-Ḥimṣī that the Messenger of Allah ﷺ said, 'Whoever is given a third of the Qur'an has been given a third of Prophethood. Whoever is given two-thirds of the Qur'an has been given two-thirds of Prophethood. Whoever recites all of the Qur'an has been given all of Prophethood although he has not received any revelation. On the Day of Rising he will be told, "Recite and ascend." He will recite an *āyah* and rise a degree until he finishes what he knows of the Qur'an. Then he will be told, "Take," and he will take. Then he will be asked, "Do you know what is in your hands? Eternity is in your right hand and bliss in your left."'

Idrīs ibn Khalaf related from Ismā'īl ibn 'Ayyāsh from Tammām from al-Ḥasan that the Messenger of Allah ﷺ said, 'Whoever takes a third of the Qur'an and acts on it has taken a third of Prophethood. Whoever takes half of the Qur'an and acts on it has taken half of Prophethood. Whoever takes all of the Qur'an has taken all of Prophethood.'

Muḥammad ibn Yaḥyā al-Marwazī related from Muḥammad ibn Sa'dān from al-Ḥusayn ibn Muḥammad from Ḥafṣ from Kathīr ibn Zādhān from 'Āṣim ibn Ḍamrah from 'Alī that the Messenger of Allah ﷺ said, 'If someone reads the Qur'an, recites it and memorises it, Allah will admit him to the Garden and let him intercede for all the people of his family for whom the Fire is mandatory.' Umm 'd-Dardā' said, 'I visited 'Ā'ishah and asked her, "What is the excellence of the one who recites the Qur'an over the one who does not recite it among those who enter the Garden?" 'Ā'ishah replied, "The number of the *āyahs* of the Qur'an is according to the number of degrees of the Garden. No one will enter the Garden better than the one who recites the Qur'an."' Abū Muḥammad Makkī mentioned it.

Ibn 'Abbās said, 'If anyone recites the Qur'an and follows what is in it, Allah has guided him out of misguidance and will protect him on the Day of Rising from an evil reckoning. That is because Allah says, "*All those who follow My guidance will not go astray and will not be miserable.*" (20:121)' Ibn 'Abbās also said, 'Allah has guaranteed that the one who follows the Qur'an will not go astray in this world nor be wretched in the Next.' Makkī also mentioned that. Al-Layth said, 'It was said that mercy does not come quicker to anyone than to the one who listens to the Qur'an, according to the words of the Almighty, "*When the Qur'an is recited, listen to it and be silent so that hopefully you will gain mercy.*" (7:204)' The word 'hopefully' makes it mandatory for Allah.'

In the *Musnad* of Abū Dāwūd aṭ-Ṭayālisī, which is the first *Musnad* composed in Islam, it is reported from 'Abdullāh ibn 'Amr that the Messenger of Allah ﷺ said, 'Anyone who stands [in prayer] for ten *āyah*s will not be written among the heedless. Anyone who stands for a hundred *āyah*s will be written among the obedient. Anyone who stands for a thousand *āyah*s will be written among those with heaps [*qinṭārs*] of reward.' There are many traditions about this, and what we have mentioned is adequate. Allah is the One who grants success in guidance.

How to recite the Book of Allah and what is disliked and forbidden in respect of it, and people's disagreement about that

Al-Bukhārī transmitted that Qatādah said, 'I asked Anas about the recitation of the Messenger of Allah ﷺ and he said, "He would lengthen syllables when he recited, '*In the Name of Allah, the All-Merciful, Most Merciful.*' He would extend the name 'Allah', extend 'ar-Raḥmān' (the All-Merciful) and extend 'ar-Raḥīm' (the Most Merciful)."' At-Tirmidhī reported that Umm Salamah said, 'The Messenger of Allah ﷺ used to put stops in his recitation. He would say, "*Praise be to Allah, the Lord of the worlds,*" and stop, "*the All-Merciful, Most Merciful,*" and stop. Then he would recite, "*Master of the Day of Repayment.*"' He said that it is a *gharīb* hadith. Abū Dāwūd transmitted a similar hadith.

It is related that the Prophet ﷺ said, 'The person with the best voice is the one that you see fears Allah Almighty when he recites.' It is related that Ziyād an-Numayrī came with the reciters to Anas ibn Mālik and was told to recite. He raised his voice and intoned. He had a loud voice and Anas uncovered his face, as he had a black cloth over it, and exclaimed,

'You! What is this you are doing?' When he saw something he objected to, he would remove the cloth from his face.

It is related that Qays ibn 'Ubbād said, 'The Companions of the Messenger of Allah ﷺ used to dislike raising the voice in dhikr.' Those who disliked raising the voice in recitation of the Qur'an included Sa'īd ibn al-Musayyab, Sa'īd ibn Jubayr, al-Qāsim ibn Muḥammad, al-Ḥasan, Ibn Sīrīn, an-Nakha'ī and others. Mālik ibn Anas and Aḥmad ibn Ḥanbal also disliked it. All of them disliked raising the voice with the Qur'an and intoning it. It is related that Sa'īd ibn al-Musayyab heard 'Umar ibn 'Abd al-'Azīz leading the people and he intoned in his recitation. Sa'īd sent a message to him saying, 'May Allah put you right! Imams should not recite like that.' So 'Umar stopped singing. Al-Qāsim ibn Muḥammad said, 'A man recited in the mosque of the Prophet ﷺ and intoned and al-Qāsim objected to that. He said, 'Allah Almighty says, "*Truly it is a Mighty Book. Falsehood cannot reach it from before it or behind it.*" (41:40-41)' Mālik related that he was asked about *nabr* (raising the pitch of the voice) when reciting the Qur'an in the prayer, and he disliked that strongly and objected to the raising the pitch of the voice in recitation. Ibn al-Qāsim related from him that he was asked about melody in the prayer and he said, 'I do not like it.' He said, 'It is a kind of singing which they do and for which they are paid money.'

One group permit raising the voice in the Qur'an and intoning it. That is because, when someone beautifies his voice when reciting it, it settles more deeply in the selves and the hearts listen more to it. They find evidence in the words of the Prophet ﷺ, 'Adorn the Qur'an with your voices.' Al-Barā' ibn 'Āzib related it and Abū Dāwūd and an-Nasā'ī transmitted it. The Prophet ﷺ said, 'He who does not sing the Qur'an is not one of us.' Muslim transmitted it. There is also what Abū Mūsā told the Prophet ﷺ: 'If I had known that you listened to my recitation, I would have beautified it for you.' 'Abdullāh ibn Mughaffal said, 'In a journey in the year of the Conquest, the Messenger of Allah ﷺ recited Sūrat al-Fatḥ on his mount and he used a quavering tone in his recitation.' Some of those who believed this were Abū Ḥanīfah and his people, ash-Shāfi'ī, Ibn al-Mubārak and an-Naḍr ibn Shumayl. It is the choice of aṭ-Ṭabarī, Abu-l-Ḥasan ibn Baṭṭāl, Qāḍī Abū Bakr ibn al-'Arabī and others.

The first position is sounder because of what we already mentioned and will mention. As for using the first hadith as evidence, it is not apparent. It is an example of the reversal of the normal order and in fact means, 'Adorn your voices with the Qur'an.' Al-Khaṭṭābī said, 'That is how more than one of the Imams of hadith have explained it, saying it is reversal.' Ma'mar related that from Manṣūr from Ṭalḥah.

Al-Khaṭṭābī related from al-Barā' that the Messenger of Allah ﷺ said, 'Adorn the Qur'an with your voices.' He said, 'It means persist in its recitation and employ your voices to do it and take it as a sign and adornment.' It is said that it means to encourage people to recite the Qur'an and persist in it. It is related from Abū Hurayrah that he heard the Messenger of Allah ﷺ say, 'Adorn your voices with the Qur'an.' It is related that 'Umar said, 'Make your voices good with the Qur'an.'

This is what the words of the Prophet ﷺ are referring to when he said, 'The one who does not sing the Qur'an is not one of us,' meaning 'the one who does not make his voice good with the Qur'an is not one of us.' That is how 'Abdullāh ibn Abī Mulaykah interpreted it. 'Abd al-Jabbār ibn al-Wird said that he heard Ibn Abī Mulaykah say that 'Abdullāh ibn Abī Yazīd said, 'Abū Lubābah passed us and we followed him until he went into his house. He was a man of shabby appearance. I heard him say, "I heard the Messenger of Allah ﷺ say, 'He who does not sing the Qur'an is not one of us.'"' 'Abd al-Jabbār said, 'I asked Ibn Abī Mulaykah, "Abū Muḥammad, what do you think of the one who does not have a good voice?" He replied, "He makes it as good as he can."' Abū Dāwūd mentioned it.

This is also the meaning of Abū Mūsā's words to the Prophet ﷺ: 'If I had known that you were listening to my recitation, I would have made my voice good in the Qur'an, adorned it and used *tartīl* (slow recitation).' This indicates that he was quick in his recitation with a good natural voice. If he had known that the Prophet ﷺ was listening, he would have extended his recitation and used *tartīl* as he usually did when he recited to the Messenger of Allah ﷺ. He used to do that in order to increase the beauty of his voice when reciting.

We seek refuge with Allah from interpreting what the Messenger of Allah ﷺ said as meaning that the Qur'an can be adorned by voices or anything else! Whoever interprets it in this way has committed something terrible in saying that the Qur'an is in need of someone to adorn it. It is Light, Illumination, and the Highest Adornment for the one who wears its splendour and is illuminated by its light. It is said that the command to adorn means to learn the readings and to adorn them with our voices. That implies: 'adorn the recitation with your voices,' since '*qur'ān*' means recitation as Allah says, '*The recitation (qur'ān) of dawn.*' (17:78) According to this interpretation, it is valid that it simply means 'to recite' as we made clear. It is as is reported in *Ṣaḥīḥ Muslim* that 'Abdullāh ibn 'Amr said, 'There are some shayṭāns imprisoned in the sea whom Solomon chained. It will soon be the time when they will emerge and recite something (*qur'ān*) to people.'

It is said that the word understood as 'singing' (*yataghannā*) comes from *istighnā'*, 'not having any need', not from *ghinā'* (singing). This was the interpretation adopted by Sufyān ibn 'Uyaynah and Wakī' ibn al-Jarrāḥ. Sufyān related that from Sa'd ibn Abī Waqqāṣ. Another point is also related from Sufyān that Isḥāq ibn Rāhwayh mentioned, which is that it means 'to be enriched and without need of other words'. This is the interpretation preferred by al-Bukhārī when he dealt with the verse, *'Is it not enough for them that We have sent down to you the Book which is recited to them?'* (29:51) What is meant by being enriched by the Qur'an is not being in need of the history of the nations. Interpreters have said that.

It is said that '*yataghannā*' means to display sorrow. In other words sorrow should appear in the reciter when he reads and recites. It does not come from '*ghunyah*' (being able to dispense with) because a different form of the verb would have been used for that. A group of scholars believed that, including Imam Ibn Ḥibbān al-Bustī. Their evidence was what Muṭarrif ibn 'Abdullāh ibn ash-Shikhkhīr related from his father: 'I came to the Messenger of Allah ﷺ while he was praying and his chest was heaving like a cauldron from weeping.' They said, 'This report makes it clear that what is meant is displaying sorrow. This is also supported by what the Imams related from 'Abdullāh: "The Prophet ﷺ said, 'Recite to me.' So I recited Sūrat an-Nisā' to him until I reached the *āyah*, *'How will it be when We bring a witness from every nation and bring you as a witness against them?'* (4:41) I saw his eyes overflowing with tears."'

These are four interpretations and none of them indicate that recitation is done with tunes or quavering voices. Abū Sa'īd al-A'rābī said about 'He who does not sing the Qur'an is not one of us': 'The Arabs were keen on singing and using verse in most of what they said. When the Qur'an was revealed, they wanted to use the Qur'an as their chant instead of singing, and the Prophet said this.'

The fifth interpretation is what some claim as evidence for quavering and singing. 'Umar ibn Shabbah said, 'I told Abū 'Āsim about Ibn 'Uyaynah's interpretation regarding "singing" meaning "being free of need" and he said, "Ibn 'Uyaynah did not do well."' Ash-Shāfi'ī was asked about the interpretation of Ibn 'Uyaynah and said, 'I know better than this. If the Prophet ﷺ had meant not having need, he would have said it. He said, "singing" and so we know that he meant singing.' Aṭ-Ṭabarī said, 'What is known in our view is that in the language of the Arabs *taghannin* is singing, which is using a good voice with quavering. It is as a poet said:

Sing the poem whenever you declaim it.
Singing (*ghinā'*) this poetry is the arena.'

He said, 'As for those who claim that it means "being without need", that is not part of the language and poetry of the Arabs. We do not know any of the people of knowledge who said that.'

In respect of what aṭ-Ṭabarī claimed about *taghannā* not meaning *istighnā'* in Arabic, al-Jawharī stated what we mentioned as did al-Harawī. There is nothing to prevent it meaning *istighnā'*, as it is indeed more appropriate to accept that which is related from a great Companion as Sufyān reported. Ibn Wahb said about Sufyān, 'I have not seen anyone with better knowledge of the interpretation of hadiths than Sufyān ibn 'Uyaynah.'

A sixth interpretation is what has been narrated in the form of an addition in *Ṣaḥīḥ Muslim,* which is that Abū Hurayrah heard the Messenger of Allah ﷺ say, 'Allah does not listen to anything so gladly as He listens to a Prophet with a good voice chanting the Qur'an aloud.' Aṭ-Ṭabarī said, 'If it had been as Ibn 'Uyaynah said, there would be no point in mentioning a good voice and aloud.' The word 'aloud' can be part of the words of the Prophet ﷺ, Abū Hurayrah or someone else. If it is the first, which is unlikely, it is evidence of lack of warbling (*taṭrīb*) and quavering because he did not say that. He said 'aloud', meaning so that he and those around him can hear him, as the Prophet ﷺ said to someone he heard raising his voice in the *shahādah*, 'People! Be kind to yourselves. You are not calling out to someone dead or absent.' So there is no evidence for what they claim. Some of our scholars preferred this interpretation, saying that it is the most likely because the Arabs use the term translated as 'singing out' for the one who raises his voice and directs it to someone absent even if it had no tune. He said, 'This is the explanation of the Companion, and he knows their manner of speaking far better.'

Abu-l-Ḥasan ibn Baṭṭāl argues for the school of ash-Shāfi'ī and says, 'The removal of the difficulty regarding this question is found in what Ibn Abī Shaybah reported from Zayd ibn al-Ḥubāb from Mūsā ibn 'Alī ibn Rabāḥ from his father that 'Uqbah ibn 'Āmir said that the Messenger of Allah ﷺ said, 'Learn the Qur'an, sing it and write it. By the One who has my soul in His hand, it is more likely to escape than a camel from the hobble.' Our scholars said, 'Even if this hadith has a sound *isnād*, what is known absolutely and definitively refutes it: the recitation of the Qur'an has reached us *mutawātir* from many shaykhs, generation after generation back to the noble era and to the Messenger of Allah ﷺ, and there was no making of tunes or intoning (*taṭrīb*) related by them, whereas they go into depth regarding the pronunciation of the letters, *maddah*, *idghām*, *iẓhār* and other types of recitation.'

Furthermore, in quavering and intoning, there is putting a *hamzah* on what does not have a *hamzah* and a lengthening of what should not be lengthened. So the single *alif* will be made into two *alif*s and one *wāw* into two. That leads to an increase in the Qur'an which is forbidden. If that occurs in a place where there is *hamzah*, they make several *hamzah*s. It may be said that 'Abdullāh ibn Mughaffal said that the Messenger of Allah ﷺ recited on his camel in the Year of the Conquest of Makkah (8/630) and quavered, which al-Bukhārī mentioned. He said, describing it, '*ā, ā, ā*' three times. That may mean *ishbā'* which is lengthening the vowel of the *maddah* in its proper place.

It is also possible that the story of his voice has to do with the rocking of his camel, as it happens to someone in a loud voice when he is riding and his voice tightens and is cut because of the rocking of the camel. Since this is possible, then it cannot be considered as evidence. Ḥāfiẓ Abū Sa'īd 'Abd al-Ghanī ibn Sa'īd transmitted from the hadith of Qatādah from 'Abd ar-Raḥmān ibn Abī Bakr who reported that his father said, 'The recitation of the Messenger of Allah ﷺ was extended (*madd*) but there was no quavering (*tarjī'*).' Ibn Jurayj reported that Ibn 'Abbās said, 'The Messenger of Allah had a *mu'adhdhin* who intoned. The Messenger of Allah ﷺ said, "The *adhān* should be easy and smooth (i.e. without trilling). If your *adhān* is not easy and smooth, then do not give the *adhān*."' Ad-Dāraquṭnī transmitted it in the *Sunan*. If the Prophet ﷺ forbade it in the *adhān*, it is more likely that he would not permit it in the Qur'an, which is preserved by the All-Merciful, as Allah says, '*It is We who have sent down the Reminder and We will preserve it*' (15:9) and '*Falsehood cannot reach it from before it or behind it – it is a revelation from One Who is All-Wise, Praiseworthy.*' (41:42)

This disagreement regarding recitation is a result of the meaning of the Qur'an not being understood due to the echoing of sounds and the great amount of quavering. If the matter goes further so that the meaning cannot be understood, then that is agreed to be forbidden. This is done by reciters in the towns of Egypt who recite before kings and at funerals and receive wages and stipends for doing so. Their effort is misguided and their action is nullified. By so doing they open the way to the alteration of the Book of Allah and it makes it easy for them to be bold against Allah by adding to His revelation what was not in it out of ignorance in their *dīn*, deviation from the Sunnah of their Prophet ﷺ, rejecting the course of the righteous Salaf in respect of that matter, and longing for what shayṭān has made seem attractive in respect of what they do. They 'suppose that they are doing good' while they compound their error and play with the Book of Allah. We belong to Allah and to Him we are returning. The Truthful One ﷺ reported that that would happen and so it is as he ﷺ reported it would be.

Imam Ḥāfiẓ Abu-l-Ḥusayn Razīn and Abū 'Abdullāh at-Tirmidhī al-Ḥakīm in *Nawādir al-uṣūl* reported the hadith transmitted by Ḥudhayfah in which the Messenger of Allah ﷺ said, 'Recite the Qur'an with the tunes and voices of the Arabs and beware of the tunes of the people of passionate love and the tunes of the People of the two Books [meaning the Torah and Gospel]. After you will come a people who make their voices quaver while reciting the Qur'an, as is done in singing and wailing. That will not go beyond their throats. Their hearts are tempted, and attracting the hearts of those who admire them is what really concerns them.' 'Tunes' refers to intoning, making the voice quaver and being good in recitation, poetry and singing.

Our scholars state that this is like those of the reciters of our time who do that before prayers and in gatherings, using foreign tunes which the Prophet ﷺ forbade. Quavering (*tarjī'*) in recitation is to repeat the letters like the Christians do. *Tartīl* in reciting the Qur'an is to recite slowly and deliberately, and to make the letters and vowels clear. It is like the petals of the daisy. It is desirable when reciting the Qur'an. Allah says, '*Recite the Qur'an distinctly.*' (73:4) Umm Salamah was asked about the recitation and prayer of the Prophet ﷺ and she said, 'What do you have to do with his prayer! He prayed and then slept the amount he prayed. Then he prayed the amount he slept and then he slept the amount he prayed until morning.' Then she described his recitation, which was an explanatory recitation, letter by letter. An-Nasā'ī, Abū Dāwūd and at-Tirmidhī transmitted it as being sound *ḥasan gharīb*.

Cautioning the people of the Qur'an and scholars against showing off

Allah Almighty says: '*Worship Allah and do not associate anything with Him*' (4:36) and the Almighty also says: '*So let him who hopes to meet his Lord act rightly and not associate anyone in the worship of his Lord.'* (18:105). Muslim reported from Abū Hurayrah that he heard the Messenger of Allah ﷺ say, 'The first of people to be judged on the Day of Rising will be a man who was martyred. He will be brought forward and will be informed of the blessings he had and will acknowledge them. Allah will ask, "What did you do with them?" He will say, "I fought for You until I was martyred." Allah will say, "You lie. Rather you fought so it would be said, 'A brave man!' And so it was said." Then the command will be given and he will be dragged on his face until he is thrown into the Fire. There will also be a man who studied knowledge and taught it and recited the Qur'an. He will be brought and informed of his blessings which he will acknowledge. Allah will say, "What did you do with them?" He will reply, "I studied knowledge and taught it and I recited the Qur'an for Your sake." Allah will say, "You lie. Rather you studied so that it would be said, 'A scholar!' and you recited so that it would be said, 'He is a reciter!' And so it was said." Then the command will be given and he will be dragged on his face until he is thrown into the Fire. There will also be a man to whom Allah gave a lot of wealth and all sorts of property. He will be brought and informed of his blessings which he will acknowledge. Allah will ask, "What did you do with them?" He will answer, "There was no path in which You like spending to be done but that I spent in it for Your sake." Allah will say, "You lie. Rather you did it so that it would be said, 'He is generous.' and so it was said." Then the command will be given and he will be dragged on his face until he is thrown into the Fire.'

At-Tirmidhī said about this hadith: 'The Messenger of Allah ﷺ then knelt and said, 'Abū Hurayrah, these three will be the first of Allah's creation to be burned by the Fire on the Day of Rising.' Abū Hurayrah's name was either 'Abdullāh or 'Abd ar-Raḥmān. He said, 'I received my *kunyah*, Abū Hurayrah, because I carried a kitten in my sleeve. The Messenger of Allah ﷺ saw me and asked, "What is this?" I said, "A cat (*hirrah*)," and he said, "Abū Hurayrah!"' Ibn 'Abd al-Barr said, 'This hadith is about someone who does not intend to please Allah by his action and his knowledge. It is related that the Prophet ﷺ said, "If someone seeks knowledge for other than the sake of Allah or intends it for other than the sake of Allah, he should take his seat in the Fire."'

In the *Raqā'iq*, Ibn al-Mubārak transmitted from al-'Abbās ibn 'Abd al-Muṭṭalib that the Messenger of Allah ﷺ said, 'This *dīn* will be victorious until it crosses the sea and until you plunge into the sea with horses in the Way of Allah Almighty. Then there will come a people who recite the Qur'an. When they recite it, they will say, "Who reads more than us? Who knows more than us?"' Then he turned to his Companions and said, 'Do you think that there will be any good in those?' 'No,' they replied. He said, 'Those are from you and those are from this Community and those are the fuel of the Fire.' Abū Dāwūd and at-Tirmidhī transmitted that the Messenger of Allah ﷺ said, 'Anyone who learns knowledge which should be learned for the sake of Allah, the Mighty and Majestic, only to obtain by it goods of this world, will not experience the scent of the Garden on the Day of Rising.' At-Tirmidhī said it is a *ḥasan* hadith.

It is related from Abū Hurayrah that the Messenger of Allah ﷺ said, 'Seek refuge with Allah from the Pit of Sorrow.' They asked, 'Messenger of Allah, what is the Pit of Sorrow?' He replied, 'It is a valley in Hell from which Hell seeks refuge a hundred times a day.' He was asked, 'Messenger of Allah, who will enter it?' He replied, 'Those who recite to show off their actions.' He said that it is a *gharīb* hadith. In the book of Asad ibn Mūsā it is reported that the Prophet ﷺ said, 'There is a valley in Hell, and Hell seeks refuge from the evil of that valley seven times a day. In that valley is a pit, and Hell and that valley seek refuge from the evil of that pit. In that pit is a serpent and Hell, the valley and the pit seek refuge with Allah from the evil of that serpent seven times. Allah has prepared it for the wretched among those who know the Qur'an but disobey Allah.'

So the one who knows the Qur'an and seeks knowledge should fear Allah regarding himself and act sincerely for Allah. If he does anything which is disliked, he should hasten to repent and begin to show sincerity in his goal and his actions. The one who knows the Qur'an must guard himself even more carefully than others, as he has a wage which others do not have. At-Tirmidhī transmitted that Abu-d-Dardā' reported that the Messenger of Allah ﷺ said, 'Allah revealed in one of the Books to one of the Prophets, "Warn those who seek understanding for other than the *dīn* and learn for other than action and seek this world by the deeds of the Next World. They wear sheepskins in front of people to give the impression of meekness while their hearts are like the hearts of wolves. Their tongues are sweeter than honey while their hearts are more bitter than aloes. They try to deceive Me and make light of Me. I will send them trials which will leave even the forbearing bewildered."'

Aṭ-Ṭabarī transmitted in *Adab an-nufūs* from Abū Kurayb Muḥammad ibn al-'Alā' from al-Muḥāribī from 'Amr ibn 'Āmir al-Bajalī from Ibn Ṣadaqah that one of the Companions of the Prophet said that the

Messenger of Allah ﷺ said, 'Do not try to deceive Allah. If anyone tries to deceive Allah, Allah will deceive him. It is his own self which is deceived if only he were aware.' They asked, 'Messenger of Allah, how can someone try to deceive Allah?' He replied, 'By doing what Allah has commanded while seeking other than Him by it. Fear showing-off. It is *shirk*. The one who shows off will be summoned before witnesses on the Day of Rising by four names which he is called: "O unbeliever! O loser! O perfidious! O deviant! Your actions are lost and your reward is nullified. You have no share today. Seek your reward from those you acted for, O impostor!"

It is reported from 'Alqamah that 'Abdullāh ibn Mas'ūd said, 'How will you feel when you are enveloped by a trial in which children grow old, the old become senile and people act according to an innovated sunnah? When any of it is changed, it will be said, "The sunnah has been changed."' He was asked, 'When will that be, Abū 'Abd ar-Raḥmān?' He replied, 'When your reciters are many and your *fuqahā'* are few, and your leaders are many and your trusted ones are few, and this world is sought through the actions of the Next World and people learn *fiqh* for other than the *dīn*.' Sufyān ibn 'Uyaynah said, 'I heard that Ibn 'Abbās said, "If those who know the Qur'an had taken it as it should be taken and in the way that is proper for it, Allah would love them. But they seek this world by it and so Allah hates them and they are indulgent with people."' It is related from Abū Ja'far Muḥammad ibn 'Alī about the words of the Almighty, '*They will be bundled headfirst into it, they and the misled*' (26:94), 'This refers to people who describe the truth and justice with their tongues and then oppose it by espousing something other than that.'

What someone who knows the Qur'an must do and not neglect to do

The first thing is to be sincere in seeking it for the sake of Allah as we mentioned. You should make yourself recite the Qur'an night and day, in the prayer or outside the prayer, so that you do not forget it. Muslim transmitted from Ibn 'Umar that the Messenger of Allah ﷺ said, 'The example of the one who knows the Qur'an is like the one who has hobbled camels. If he takes care of them, he will keep them. If he releases them, they will go off. When the one who knows the Qur'an stands and recites it night and day, he remembers it. If he does not do that, he forgets it.' So someone who knows Qur'an must praise Allah, be thankful for His blessing, remember Him, rely on Him, seek His help, desire Him and cling to Him. He must remember death and prepare for it. He should fear his wrong actions and hope for his Lord's pardon. When his health is good his fear should be stronger since he does not know what his seal will be. When he is close to dying, his hope should be stronger on account of his good opinion of Allah. The Messenger of Allah ﷺ said, 'None of you should die except with a good opinion of Allah.' This means you should think that He will have mercy on you and forgive you.

He should know the people of his time, preserve himself from the ruler, and strive to save himself and save his life, having to hand what he can of the goods of this world, striving for himself in that as much as he can. His greatest concern should be scrupulousness in his *dīn*, fearfulness of Allah and watchful awareness of Him regarding what He commands and forbids. Ibn Mas'ūd said, 'The one who recites the Qur'an should be known by his nights when people are asleep and his days when people are not fasting, his weeping when people laugh, his silence when people delve into improper matters, his humility when they are arrogant and his sorrow when they are happy.' 'Abdullāh ibn 'Amr said, 'The one who knows the Qur'an should not delve with those who delve, nor be ignorant with the ignorant, but he should pardon and overlook by the right of the Qur'an because inside of him are the words of Allah Almighty. He must protect himself from doubtful paths and laugh little and speak little in the gatherings of Qur'an and elsewhere concerning anything in which there is no benefit. He must be forbearing and grave.'

He should be humble to the poor and avoid arrogance and vanity. He should withdraw from this world and its people if he fears temptation for himself, and should abandon argumentation and dispute. He should make an effort to be kind and show proper manners. He should be with those from whose evil he is safe, whose good he hopes for and from whose injury he is safe. He should not listen to those who slander in his presence and should keep the company of those who lead him to what is good and direct him to truthfulness and noble character, those who adorn him and do not sully him.

He must learn the rulings of the Qur'an and understand what Allah means and what He mandates. Then he will benefit from what he reads and act by what he recites. How vile is the one who knows the Qur'an and recites its obligations and rulings by heart but does not understand what he recites! How can the one who does not understand what it means act? How ugly it is that he is asked about the *fiqh* of what he recites but does not know it! The metaphor of someone with a state like this is only that of '*a donkey who carries volumes*' (62:5).

He should know the Makkan from the Madinan *sūrahs* so that by that he can distinguish between what Allah told His slaves at the beginning of Islam and what was recommended for them at the end, what He made obligatory for them at the beginning of Islam and those obligations He added to it at the end. The Madinan abrogates the Makkan in most of the Qur'an. It is not possible for the Makkan to abrogate the Madinan because the abrogated was revealed before the abrogating. Part of his perfection is to know the *i'rāb* (inflection/grammar) and unusual words. That is part of what will make it easy for him to know what he reads and will remove doubt from him in what he recites.

Abū Ja'far aṭ-Ṭabarī said, 'I heard al-Jarmī say, "For thirty years, I have been giving people *fatwās* concerning *fiqh* taken from the book of Sībawayh [i.e. based on grammar]."' Muḥammad ibn Yazīd said, 'That was because Abū 'Umar al-Jarmī knew hadiths. When he learned the book of Sībawayh, he learned *fiqh* from hadith since it is from the book of Sībawayh that he learned investigation and *tafsīr*. Then he looked into the sunnahs which are firmly transmitted from the Messenger of Allah ﷺ. It is by means of them that the seeker attains to what Allah means in His Book and that opens up for him the judgments of the Qur'an. Aḍ-Ḍaḥḥāk said about the words of the Almighty, "*Be people of the Lord because of your knowledge of the Book*" (3:79), "It is a duty for whoever learns the Qur'an to be a *faqīh*."'

Ibn Abi-l-Ḥawārī said, 'A group of us went to Fuḍayl ibn 'Iyāḍ in 185 AH and stopped at his door, but he did not give us permission to enter. One of the people said, "If he comes out for anything, he will come out to recitation of the Qur'an." So we ordered a reciter to recite and he appeared to us at a window. We said, "Peace be upon you and the mercy of Allah." He said, "And peace upon you." We asked, "How are you, Abū 'Alī?" He replied, "I am in well-being from Allah and harm from you. What you are doing is something new in Islam. We belong to Allah and are returning to Him! This is not how to seek knowledge! We used to go to the shaykhs and would not see ourselves worthy of sitting with them. We sat below them and eavesdropped. When a hadith was given, we would ask them to repeat it and we would retain it. You seek knowledge with ignorance. You waste the Book of Allah. If you had sought the Book of Allah, you would have found in it healing for what you want." We said, "We have studied the Qur'an." He said, "Your study of the Qur'an is work enough for your lives and the lives of your children!" We asked, "How, Abū 'Alī?" He replied, "You will not learn the Qur'an until you know its *i'rāb* (syntax), its *muḥkam* from its *mutashābih*, and its abrogating from its abrogated. When you know that, then you will have no need of the words of Fuḍayl and Ibn 'Uyaynah." Then he said, "I seek refuge with Allah, the All-Hearing, All-Knowing from the Accursed Shayṭān. *In the Name of Allah, the All-Merciful, the Most Merciful. 'O mankind! An admonition has come to you from your Lord and also healing for what is in the breasts and guidance and mercy for the believers. Say: "It is the favour of Allah and His mercy that should be the cause of their rejoicing. That is better than anything they accumulate."""* (10:57-58)'

When a reader of the Qur'an obtains these ranks, he will be fluent in the Qur'an and know the Discrimination. He will be close to the one who brings him close to it. He will not benefit from anything we have mentioned until he has a sincere intention for Allah when he seeks it, or continues to have a sincere intention after learning it, as was already stated. A seeker of knowledge may begin by desiring reputation and honour in the *dīn*. Then his acquisition of knowledge continues until it is clear to him that he has erred in his belief, and so he repents of that and makes his intention sincere for Allah. He benefits from that and improves his state. Al-Ḥasan said, 'We used to seek knowledge for the sake of this world and it dragged us to the Next World.' Sufyān ath-Thawrī said that. Ḥabīb ibn Abī Thābit said, 'We sought this matter and we had no intention in respect of it. The intention came afterwards.'

The syntax of the Qur'an, learning it and studying it, and the reward for the one who recites the Qur'an with proper inflections

Abū Bakr al-Anbārī said, 'The Prophet ﷺ, his Companions and their Followers all mention the excellence of proper understanding of the syntax of the Qur'an and the encouragement to learn it and censure and dislike poor grammatical understanding. This obliges the reciters of the Qur'an to strive to learn it.'

One aspect of that is in what is related by Yaḥyā ibn Sulaymān aḍ-Ḍabbī from Muḥammad ibn Sa'īd from Abū Mu'āwiyah from 'Abdullāh ibn Sa'īd al-Maqburī from his father from his grandfather from Abū Hurayrah who reported that the Prophet ﷺ said, 'Use the proper syntax in the Arabic of the Qur'an and search out its unusual words.' My father related from Ibrāhīm ibn al-Haytham from Ādam ibn Abī Iyās and Abu-ṭ-Ṭayyib al-Marwazī from 'Abd al-'Azīz ibn Abī Rawwād from Nāfi' from Ibn ‘Umar that the Messenger of Allah ﷺ said, ‘If someone recites the Qur’an without its correct grammar, an angel is entrusted to him to write for him, as it was revealed, ten good deeds for every letter. When he uses correct grammar for some of it and fails to do so for some of it, two angels are entrusted who write down for every letter twenty good deeds. If he inflects it correctly, four angels are entrusted to him to write down seventy good deeds for every letter.’ Juwaybir related that aḍ-Ḍaḥḥāk said that ‘Abdullāh ibn Mas‘ūd said, ‘Recite the Qur’an well and adorn it with your voices and employ its correct syntax. It is Arabic and Allah loves the correct syntax to be employed.’ Mujāhid reported that Ibn ‘Umar said, ‘Use correct syntax in the Qur’an.’

Muḥammad ibn ‘Abd ar-Raḥmān ibn Zayd related that Abū Bakr and ‘Umar said, ‘We prefer some knowledge of the syntax of the Qur’an to simply memorising its letters.’ Ash-Sha‘bī reported that ‘Umar said, ‘Anyone who recites the Qur’an with its syntax has the reward with Allah of a martyr.’ Makḥūl said, ‘We were told that anyone who recites with correct syntax has double the reward of someone who recites without it.’ Ibn Jurayj related from ‘Aṭā’ that Ibn ‘Abbās reported that the Messenger of Allah ﷺ said, ‘Love the Arabs for three reasons: because I am an Arab, because the Qur’an is in Arabic and because the language of the people of the Garden will be Arabic.’ Sufyān related that Abū Ḥamzah said, ‘Al-Ḥasan was asked about people studying Arabic and he said, “They do well. They learn the language of their Prophet ﷺ.”’ Al-Ḥasan was told, ‘We have an imam who uses ungrammatical Arabic.’ He said, ‘Dismiss him.’

Ibn Abī Mulaykah said, ‘A Bedouin arrived in Madīnah in the time of ‘Umar ibn al-Khaṭṭāb and asked, “Who will recite some of what was revealed to Muḥammad ﷺ?” A man recited Sūrat at-Tawbah to him. He said, “Allah is free of the idolaters and His Messenger” using the genitive for Messenger (*rasūlihi*). The Bedouin said, “Allah is free of His Messenger? If Allah is free of His Messenger, we are more free of him.” ‘Umar heard what the Bedouin had said so he summoned him and said, “Bedouin, are you free of the Messenger of Allah?” He replied, “Amīr al-Mu’minīn, I came to Madīnah with no knowledge of the Qur’an. I asked someone to recite it to me and he recited this Sūrat at-Tawbah and said, ‘Allah is free of the idolaters and His Messenger.’ So I said, ‘Allah is free of His Messenger? If Allah is free of His Messenger, we are more free of him.’” ‘Umar said, “That is not how it is, Bedouin.” He asked, “How is it then, Amīr al-Mu’minīn?” He said, “*Allah is free of the idolaters, as is His*

Messenger (*rasūluhu*)." The Bedouin said, "We, by Allah, are more free of what Allah and His Messenger are free of!" So 'Umar ibn al-Khaṭṭāb commanded that only those who knew proper grammar should recite to people, and he commanded Abu-l-Aswad to set out the grammar.'

'Alī ibn al-Ja'd reported that he heard Shu'bah say, 'The metaphor of someone who knows the hadith but does not know Arabic is that of a donkey that has a nosebag with no fodder in it.' Ḥammād ibn Salamah said, 'The one who seeks hadith and does not learn grammar – or Arabic – is like a donkey who has a nosebag in which there is no barley.' Ibn 'Aṭiyyah said, 'The syntax of the Qur'an is a basic principle in the Sharī'ah because it is that by which its meanings, which are the Sharī'ah, are established.'

Ibn al-Anbārī said, 'The Companions of the Prophet and their Followers provide evidence for using language and poetry to explain unusual and problematic words in the Qur'an, and that demonstrates the soundness of the school of the grammarians respecting that and the falsity of those who deny that.' An element of that is what is related from 'Ubayd ibn 'Abd al-Wāḥid ibn Sharīk al-Bazzāz from Ibn Abī Maryam from Ibn Tarūkh from Usāmah from 'Ikrimah that Ibn 'Abbās said, 'When you ask me about the unusual words of Allah, look for them in poetry. Poetry is the lexicon of the Arabs.' Idrīs ibn 'Abd al-Karīm related from Khalaf from Ḥammād ibn Zayd from 'Alī ibn Zayd ibn Jud'ān who heard Sa'īd ibn Jubayr and Yūsuf ibn Mihrān mention that they heard Ibn 'Abbās being asked about something in the Qur'an and he replied. 'It means such and such. Have you not heard the poet say such-and-such?' 'Ikrimah reported that a man asked Ibn 'Abbās about the words of Allah, '*Purify your clothes.*' (74:4) He said, 'Do not put on your garment in a state of treachery.' He cited as an example the words of Ghaylān ath-Thaqafī:

Allah be praised, I did not put on a garment in treachery
nor cover up evil!

A man asked 'Ikrimah about a bastard (*zanīm*) and he said that it is the child of fornication and cited a verse:

A bastard (*zanīm*) is not known for his father
with a mother who is a harlot. He has blameworthy lineage.

He also said that *zanīm* is someone ignoble, base and a false claimant. He said:

Men competed in increasing the ignoble,
as feet increase the size of the skin.

He also said about the words of the Almighty, '*shaded by spreading branches (afnān)*' (55:48) that the gardens have shade and branches. He said, 'Do you not hear the words of the poet? He said:

Your yearning does not rouse a dove from a branch,
calling doves to the branches (*afnān*) of the boughs.
You call to the father of the chicks like a bird
with the talons of the sparrow-hawks.'

'Ikrimah reported that Ibn 'Abbās said about the words of the Almighty, '*at once they will be at as-sāhirah*' (79:14), 'It is the earth. Ubayy ibn Abi-ṣ-Ṣalt said, "They have flesh from the sea and flesh from land (*sāhirah*)."' Ibn al-Anbārī said that transmitters relate this verse:

In it is both flesh from the land (*sāhirah*) and from the sea.
What they say remains for them.

Nāfi' ibn al-Azraq said to Ibn 'Abbās, 'Tell me about the words of Allah, "*He is not subject to drowsiness (sinah) or sleep.*" (2:255) What is *sinah*?' He replied, 'Drowsiness. Zuhayr ibn Abī Sulmā said:

He was not overcome by drowsiness (*sinah*) in the long nights
and did not sleep. There is no weakness in his business.

What is reported about the excellence of *tafsīr* of the Qur'an and those who do it

Our scholars say that part of what is transmitted from the Companions and Followers about the excellence of *tafsīr* is that 'Alī ibn Abī Ṭālib mentioned Jābir ibn 'Abdullāh and described him as having knowledge. A man said to him, 'May I be your ransom! You describe Jābir as having knowledge when you are who are you are!' He replied, 'He knew the *tafsīr* of the words of Allah, "*He who has imposed the Qur'an upon you will most certainly bring you back home again.*" (28:85)' Mujāhid said, 'The dearest of creatures to Allah Almighty is the one who has the most knowledge of what is revealed.' Al-Ḥasan said, 'Allah has not revealed any *āyah* without wanting people to know why it was revealed and what it means.' Ash-Sha'bī said, 'Masrūq travelled to Basra for the *tafsīr* of an *āyah* and was told that the one who could explain it had travelled to Syria. So he made preparations and travelled to Syria to learn its *tafsīr*.'

'Ikrimah said about the words of the Almighty, '*If anyone leaves his home, making hijrah to Allah and His Messenger*' (4:99), 'I sought the name of this man "*who leaves his home, making hijrah to Allah and His Messenger*" for fourteen years until I found it.' Ibn 'Abd al-Barr said that it was Ḍamrah ibn Ḥabīb. Ibn 'Abbās said, 'I remained for two years wanting to ask 'Umar about the two women who helped each other against the Messenger of Allah ﷺ and only awe of him prevented me from asking. Finally I asked him and he replied that it was Ḥafṣah and 'Ā'ishah.' Iyās ibn Mu'āwiyah said, 'The metaphor of those who recite the Qur'an without knowing its *tafsīr* is that of some people to whom a letter comes from their king at night when they have no lamp. They are alarmed, not knowing what the letter contains. The metaphor of the one who knows the *tafsīr* is that of a man who brings them a lamp so that they can read what the letter says.'

What is reported about the one who is a bearer of the Qur'an, who he is and those who are hostile to him

Abū 'Umar said, 'It is related by various paths that the Prophet ﷺ said, "An aspect of esteem for Allah is honouring three: a just ruler, a Muslim with white hair and a bearer of the Qur'an who is neither excessive in it nor turns away from it.' Abū 'Umar said that the bearers of the Qur'an are those who know its rulings, its lawful and unlawful and act by what it contains. Anas reported that the Messenger of Allah ﷺ said, 'The Qur'an is better than everything. Whoever respects the Qur'an has respected Allah. Whoever makes light of the Qur'an has made light of the right of Allah Almighty. The bearers of the Qur'an are those who are encircled by the mercy of Allah, exalting the Word of Allah, touched by the light of Allah. Allah befriends whoever befriends them, and Allah is hostile to whoever is hostile to them; such people have made light of the right of Allah.'

The respect and esteem for the Qur'an which is mandatory for someone who recites and bears the Qur'an

In *Nawādir al-uṣūl*, at-Tirmidhī al-Ḥakīm said, 'An aspect of respect for the Qur'an is to only touch it when you are in a state of purity. Another aspect of respect for it is to recite it in a state of purity. Yet another aspect of respect for it is to use the tooth-stick (*siwāk*), clean between the teeth and make the mouth clean, as the mouth is its pathway. Yazīd ibn Abī Mālik said, "Your mouths are the pathways of the Qur'an, so purify and clean them as much as you can."

'Part of respect for it is to dress as you would dress to visit the ruler when you want to speak privately to him. Part of respect for it is to face *qiblah* when you recite it. When Abu-l-'Aliyyah recited he would put on a turban, dress, wear a cloak and face *qiblah.* Part of respect for it is to rinse your mouth when you spit. Shu'bah reported from Abū Ḥamzah from Ibn 'Abbās that he had a spittoon in front of him and when he spat, he would rinse his mouth and then begin recitation. Whenever he spat, he rinsed. Part of respect for it is that when you yawn, you should stop reciting, because when one recites, one is addressing and conversing with the Lord. Yawning is from Shayṭān. Mujāhid said, "When you yawn while reciting the Qur'an, stop reciting out of respect until you stop yawning." 'Ikrimah said, "By that he meant to respect the Qur'an."

'Part of respect for it is to seek refuge with Allah from the accursed Shayṭān when starting to recite it. You should say "*In the Name of Allah, the All-Merciful, the Most Merciful*" when beginning to recite it from the first *sūrah* or from wherever you start. Part of respect for it is that, when you begin to recite it, you should not stop for a time to speak to people without need. Part of respect for it is that you should not stop reciting it when someone interrupts you by speaking to you and mix recitation with your reply. That is because when you do that, you remove the effectiveness of the formula of seeking refuge that you uttered at the beginning. Part of respect for it is to recite it deliberately, slowly and carefully.

'Part of respect for it is to deploy your mind and intelligence in understanding what is addressed to you. Part of respect for it is to stop at an *āyah* of promise and have hope in Allah and ask Him for His bounty, and to stop at an *āyah* of warning and seek refuge with Allah from the threat. Part of respect for it is to stop at its metaphors and visualise them. Part of respect for it is to investigate its unusual words. Part of respect for it is to give every letter its due so that the words are fully articulated and then you will receive ten good deeds for every letter.

'Part of respect for it is to end its recitation by proclaiming the truthfulness of its Lord and testifying to its delivery by His Messenger ﷺ and testifying that that is true. You say:

صَدَقْتَ رَبَّنَا، وَبَلَّغَتْ رُسُلُكَ، وَنَحْنُ عَلَى ذَلِكَ مِنَ الشَّاهِدِينَ،
اللَّهُمَّ اجْعَلْنَا مِنْ شُهَدَاءِ الْحَقِّ، الْقَائِمِينَ بِالْقِسْطِ.

"You have spoken the Truth O our Lord, and His Messengers conveyed it and we testify to that. O Allah, make us among the witnesses to the Truth, establishing justice." Then you make supplication.

'Part of respect for it is that when you recite, you do not take *āyahs* piecemeal from each *sūrah* and recite them. It is related to us that the Messenger of Allah ﷺ passed by Bilāl who was reciting a little from each *sūrah* and he commanded him to recite the entire *sūrah.*

'Part of respect for it is that when you put down a copy of the Qur'an, you do not leave it open and do you not put any other book on top of it. It should always be on top of any other books, be they books of knowledge or other books. Part of respect for it is that when you recite, you put it in your lap or on top of something in front of you and do not put it on the ground. Part of respect for it is not to erase the board it is written on with spit, but rather use water. Part of respect for it is that when it is washed with water you avoid impurities from various places and in the places where it is put. That washing is respect. Some of the Salaf before us used to use that water to heal themselves. Part of respect for it is to not take a page when it is worn out and brittle out of fear for the writing. That is great coarseness. It should be erased with water.

'Part of respect for it is to not let a day pass without looking at least once at the Qur'an. Abū Mūsā used to say, "I am ashamed not to look once a day at the contract of my Lord." Part of respect for it is to give the eyes their share of it. The eye leads to the self. Between the self and the breast is a veil and the Qur'an is in the breast. When you recite it by heart the ear listens and conveys it to the self. When you look at its writing, the eye and the ear both convey it. That is more likely to achieve the conveyance. Then the eye has its share just as the ear does. Zayd ibn Aslam reported from 'Aṭā' ibn Yasār from Abū Sa'īd al-Khudrī that the Messenger of Allah ﷺ said, "Give the eyes their portion of worship." They asked. "Messenger of Allah, what is their portion of worship?" He replied, "To look at the Qur'an and reflect on it and study its wonders." Makḥūl reported from 'Ubādah ibn aṣ-Ṣāmit that the Messenger of Allah ﷺ said, "The best worship of my community is to read the Qur'an with the eyes."

'Part of respect for it is not to resort to it when offered worldly goods. 'Amr ibn Ziyād al-Ḥanẓalī related from Hushaym ibn Bashīr from al-Mughīrah that Ibrāhīm [an-Nakha'ī] used to dislike to resort to any of the Qur'an when he was offered worldly goods. That is like saying to a man who comes to you, "*You have arrived at the pre-ordained time, Mūsā*," (20:40) and like saying, "*Eat and drink with relish for what you did before in days gone by*" (69:24) when food is served, and other such things. Part of respect for it is not to say Sūrat an-Naḥl, Sūrat al-Baqarah and Sūrat an-Nisā', but to say, "The *sūrah* in which such-and-such is mentioned."'

I say that this, however, is contrary to the words of the Prophet ﷺ, "If anyone recites the two *āyah*s from the end of Sūrat al-Baqarah at night, they will be enough for him." Al-Bukhārī and Muslim transmitted it from 'Abdullāh ibn Mas'ūd.

'Part of respect for it is to not invert it, as some teachers of children do, in order to show off cleverness and fluency. That is opposition to Allah. Part of respect for it is to not exaggerate its recitation as is done by those obstinate innovators who intensify the pronunciation of the *hamzah* and pronounce words with affectation. That is an innovation which Shayṭān suggested to them that they accepted. Part of respect for it is not to recite it using musical tunes like the tunes of the people of depravity nor with the quavering of the Christians nor chanting of the monks. All of that is deviation.

'Part of respect for it is to make its letters bold. Abū Ḥukaymah reported that he used to copy out Qur'an in Kufa. 'Alī passed by him, inspected his writing and ordered, "Make your pen thicker." He said, "So I took the pen and trimmed part of it and then wrote while 'Alī was standing and looking at my writing. He said, 'Like that. Give light to it as Allah gave it light.'"

'Part of respect for it is not to compete in loudness in recitation so that it becomes spoiled for the other and he hates what he hears and it becomes like a contest. Part of respect for it is not to argue or quarrel about its recitations or say to a person, "It is not like that." Perhaps that recitation is a sound and permitted one and then you would be denying the Book of Allah.

'Part of respect for it is not to recite it in the market or in places of clamour, worthless talk, and the places where fools congregate. Do you not see that Allah Almighty mentioned the slaves of the All-Merciful and praised them because, when they pass by worthless talk, they pass by it with dignity? (cf. 25:72) This is about simply passing by those engaged in worthless talk. So how could they recite the Qur'an in the midst of worthless talk and a gathering of fools?

'Part of respect for it is not to use it as pillow or lean on it or throw it to someone when he wants it to be passed to him.

'Part of respect for it is not to make it small. ... It is reported that 'Alī said, "Do not make the Qur'an small." It is related that 'Umar ibn al-Khaṭṭāb saw a small Qur'an in the hand of a man and asked, "Who wrote it?" "I did," he replied, and then 'Umar struck him with his whip and said, "Esteem the Qur'an." It is related that the Prophet ﷺ forbade people to say, 'a little mosque or a little Qur'an" (using the diminutive).

'Part of respect for it is not to mix it with what is not part of it. Part of respect for it is not to adorn it with gold or write it in gold so that it is mixed with the adornment of this world. Mughīrah related that Ibrāhīm disliked adorning the Qur'an or writing it with gold or putting marks at the beginning of *āyahs* or making it small. It is related from Abu-d-Dardā' that the Messenger of Allah ﷺ said, "When you adorn your mosque and decorate your Qur'an, then ruin is upon you." When Ibn 'Abbās saw a Qur'an adorned with silver he said, "You tempt the thief with it. Its adornment is inside it."

'Part of respect for it is that it should not be written on the ground or on a wall as is done in modern mosques. Muḥammad ibn 'Alī ash-Shaqīqī related from his father from 'Abdullāh ibn al-Mubārak from Sufyān from Muḥammad ibn az-Zubayr who heard 'Umar ibn 'Abd al-'Azīz say, "The Messenger of Allah ﷺ passed by some writing on the ground and said to a lad of the tribe of Hudhayl, 'What is this?' He replied, 'It is from the Book of Allah. A Jew wrote it.' He said, 'May Allah curse the one who did this. Only put the Book of Allah in its proper place.'" Muḥammad ibn az-Zubayr said that 'Umar ibn 'Abd al-'Azīz saw a son of his writing the Qur'an on a wall and beat him.

'Part of respect for it is that when its writing is washed for treating an illness, it should not be poured on a rubbish heap or in a place of impurity or in a place where people walk, but in a place where people do not walk, or a hole should be dug in a pure place so that it can be poured into it, or it can be poured into a large river.

'Part of respect for it is that, whenever someone completes the recitation of the entire Qur'an, he recites some of the beginning so that it does not have the form of something abandoned. That is why when the Messenger of Allah ﷺ finished reciting, he would recite about five *āyahs* from the beginning so that it would not be in an abandoned form. Ibn 'Abbās said that a man came and asked, "Messenger of Allah, which action is best?" He replied, "You should be in a state of embarkation." "What is a state of embarkation?" he asked. He replied, "The one with the Qur'an who starts from its beginning until he reaches its end and then starts again at the beginning. Whenever he alights, he immediately travels on.'"

'It is recommended to gather your family when you finish the Qur'an. Abū Bakr al-Anbārī reported from Idrīs from Khalaf from Wakī' from Mis'ar from Qatādah that when Anas ibn Mālik finished reciting the Qur'an, he would gather his family and make supplication. Idrīs reported from Khalaf from Jarīr from Manṣūr from al-Ḥakam that when Mujāhid, 'Abdah ibn Abī Lubābah and various people were about to complete the recitation, they would summon people since mercy descends at the completion of the Qur'an. Idrīs reported from Khalaf from Hushaym from al-'Awwām that Ibrāhīm at-Taymī said, "When someone finishes the Qur'an at the beginning of the day, the angels bless him until evening. When someone finishes the Qur'an at the beginning of the night, the angels bless him until morning." He said, "They recommended that it should be finished at the beginning of the night or at the beginning of the day."

'Part of respect for it is that you should not write the refuge *sūrah*s from it and then enter the lavatory unless they are inside a covering of leather or silver or something else. Then it is as if it were inside his breast.

'Part of respect for it is that when you write it out [for medicinal purposes] and then drink it, you should say the Name of Allah for every breath and have a very strong intention. Allah will give to you according to your intention. Mujāhid said, "There is no harm in writing out the Qur'an and then having a sick person drink it." Abū Ja'far said, "If someone has hardness in his heart, he should write 'Yāsīn' on a goblet with saffron and drink it."'

I say that part of respect for it is not to say, 'What a short sūrah!' Abu-l-'Aliyyah disliked saying 'What a short or long *sūrah*'. When he heard someone say that, he would retort, 'You are smaller than it. All of the Qur'an is immense.' Abū Dāwūd related the contrary of this from the hadith of 'Amr ibn Shu'ayb from his grandfather which states that one can use those terms. 'Amr said, 'No small or long *sūrah* is part of the Mufaṣṣal.'

What is reported regarding threats against engaging in *tafsīr* of the Qur'an by means of opinion (*ra'y*) or being bold in doing that, and the ranks of the commentators

It is related that 'Ā'ishah said, 'The Messenger of Allah ﷺ did not explain the meaning of the Book of Allah except for some *āyah*s which Jibrīl explained to him.' Ibn 'Aṭiyyah said, 'The meaning of this hadith is that it is about the unseen things of the Qur'an, explaining what is undefined (*mujmal*) and the like, which there is no way to uncover except with Allah's help. An aspect of that are those unseen matters which Allah has not made known, such as the time of the Rising and the number of blasts on the Trumpet and the order of the creation of the heavens and the earth.'

At-Tirmidhī reported from Ibn 'Abbās that the Prophet ﷺ said, 'Fear attributing words to me of which you have no knowledge. Anyone who deliberately tells a lie regarding me will take his seat in the Fire. Anyone who speaks about the Qur'an from his own opinion, will take his seat in the Fire.' It is also reported from Jundub that the Messenger of Allah ﷺ said, 'Anyone who speaks about the Qur'an according to his own opinion and is right is still wrong.' This is a *gharīb* hadith which Abū Dāwūd transmitted, and one of its transmitters is questionable. Razīn added, 'Whoever speaks by his opinion and errs has disbelieved.'

Abū Bakr Muḥammad ibn Bashshār ibn Muḥammad al-Anbārī, the linguist and grammarian, said in the *Kitāb ar-radd*, 'There are two interpretations of the hadith of Ibn 'Abbās. One is that someone who speaks on problematic things (*mushkil*) in the Qur'an without proper knowledge, differing from the position of the first Companions and *Tābi'ūn*, exposes himself to the anger of Allah. The second, which is the firmer and sounder of the two, is that when someone says something about the Qur'an knowing the truth to be different, he should take his seat in the Fire.'

Regarding the hadith of Jundub, some of the people of knowledge say that 'opinion' here means 'whim'. Whoever speaks about the Qur'an according to his own whims and does not take from the Imams of the Salaf and happens to be right is still wrong since he has judged the Qur'an by something whose basis is not recognised and is not based on the position of those with expertise in traditions and transmission. Ibn 'Aṭiyyah says, 'The meaning of this is that a man is asked about a meaning of the Book of Allah and hurries to explain it by his own opinion without looking at what the scholars have said and what the rules of knowledge like syntax and fundamental principles demand.' Not included is the explanation of grammarians and linguists of its grammar and the *fuqahā'* of its meaning where each speaks by his *ijtihād* based on the rules of his own branch of knowledge and research.

This is sound and more than one scholar prefers it. The one who speaks according to what pops into his imagination and occurs to his mind without seeking evidence for it in the fundamental principles errs. Anyone who derives its meanings by basing himself on the fundamental principles, which are agreed upon, is praised.

Some scholars have said that *tafsīr* is dependent on oral transmission since Allah says, '*If you have a dispute about something, refer it back to Allah and His Messenger.*' (4:59) This is false because the prohibition against explaining the Qur'an is either that what is desired is to confine oneself to transmission and not investigate, or it is something else. It is false that what is meant is that no one should say anything about the Qur'an other than what he has heard. The Companions recited the Qur'an and differed about its interpretation in some cases. Not all of what they said was what they heard from the Prophet ﷺ. The Prophet ﷺ made supplication for Ibn 'Abbās and said, 'O Allah, give him understanding in the *dīn* and teach him interpretation.' If interpretation is confined to Revelation and Prophetic reports, what is the point of singling him out for it? This is clear and undoubted.

The prohibition against *tafsīr* applies in two instances. The first is when the interpreter voices an opinion about something on the basis of his own nature and passion and, therefore, interprets the Qur'an according to his opinion and passion in an effort to justify his position. If it had not been for that opinion and passion, that meaning about the Qur'an would not have occurred to him. This can sometimes be conscious, as in the case of someone who uses some *āyah*s of the Qur'an to prove the validity of an innovation, when he knows that that is not what is meant by the *āyah*, but his aim is to confuse his opponent. Sometimes it is done in ignorance which may happen when an *āyah* can be applied in various ways and his understanding inclines to the meaning which coincides with his position. He prefers that interpretation because of his own opinion and passion and so he interprets it according to his own opinion. If it had not been for his opinion, he would not have preferred that meaning.

Sometimes someone has a sound purpose and seeks evidence for it in the Qur'an and uses what he knows of it as evidence for what he wants to convey, like the one who calls people to strive against a hard heart. Allah says, "*Go to Pharaoh. He has overstepped the bounds.*" (20:23) He points to his heart and suggests that that is what is meant by 'Pharaoh' in this *āyah*. This kind of interpretation is used by some preachers with good motives to make their words effective and encourage their listeners. It is forbidden because it is unacceptable linguistic analogy and is not permissible. The esotericists use the same method to false purposes with the goal of deluding people and calling them to their false beliefs. They use the Qur'an according to their opinion and position in matters that they absolutely know are not meant. This is one of the aspects of *tafsīr* that is forbidden.

The second instance is when an interpreter hastens to explain the Qur'an according to the literal meaning of the Arabic without the help of transmission about what the unusual words of the Qur'an mean and what has been passed down about the ambiguous and interchangeable words, conciseness, elision, concealment and reversal of order it contains. Someone who does not have a firm grasp of the literal *tafsīr* and then sets out to derive meanings by simple understanding of Arabic often errs and joins the company of those who interpret the Qur'an according to their own opinions.

Transmission is necessary first of all in the primary *tafsīr* so that one avoids error, and then after that one employs understanding and deduction to expand on it. The unusual words, which are only understood via transmission, are numerous and one cannot hope to reach the inward before having a firm grasp of the outward. Do you not see that the Almighty says: '*We gave Thamūd the camel as a visible sign (mubṣirah) and then they mistreated her*' (17:59)? It means a visible sign, and they wronged themselves by killing it. Someone who looks at the literal Arabic might think that it means that the camel could see (*mubṣirah*) and therefore not know what they did wrong and how they wronged others and themselves. This is an example of elision and concealment. There are many such examples in the Qur'an. In cases other than these two, there is no prohibition against interpretation, and Allah knows best.

Ibn 'Aṭiyyah said, 'Most of the righteous Salaf like Sa'īd ibn al-Musayyab, 'Āmir ash-Sha'bī and others used to be overawed at the prospect of making interpretation of the Qur'an and would refrain from it out of scrupulousness and caution for themselves in spite of their perfection and precedence.' Abū Bakr al-Anbārī said, 'The imams of the Salaf were too scrupulous to explain the problematic parts of the Qur'an. One of them supposed that his *tafsīr* might not coincide with what Allah meant and so refrained from speaking. Another feared that he would become an imam in *tafsīr* and people might follow his method, when he might hesitate to explain a single letter according to his own opinion or to err about it and then his follower might say, "My imam in the *tafsīr* of the Qur'an by opinion is so-and-so, the imam of the Salaf." Ibn Abī Mulaykah said, "Abū Bakr aṣ-Ṣiddīq was asked about the *tafsīr* of a letter of the Qur'an and said, 'Which heaven will cover me and which earth will bear me? Where will I go? What will I do if I say about a letter of the Book of Allah other than what Allah Almighty meant?"'"

Ibn 'Aṭiyyah said, 'Several of the Salaf used to explain the Qur'an and caused the Muslims to continue doing that. As for the original commentators on whom they relied, there was 'Alī ibn Abī Ṭālib, and he was followed by 'Abdullāh ibn 'Abbās, who devoted himself to the subject and perfected it. He was followed by scholars like Mujāhid, Sa'īd ibn Jubayr and others. More is transmitted from him than has been preserved from 'Alī. Ibn 'Abbās said, "What I grasped of *tafsīr* of the Qur'an was from 'Alī ibn Abī Ṭālib." 'Alī used to praise the *tafsīr* of Ibn 'Abbās and encouraged people to take it from him. Ibn Mas'ūd used to say, "An excellent translator of the Qur'an is 'Abdullāh ibn 'Abbās." 'Alī said about him, "It is as if Ibn 'Abbās looks at the unseen through a fine curtain."

'He was followed up by 'Abdullāh ibn Mas'ūd, Ubayy ibn Ka'b, Zayd ibn Thābit, and 'Abdullāh ibn 'Amr ibn al-'Āṣ. All that is taken from the Companions has preference because they witnessed the Revelation and its coming down in their language. 'Āmir ibn Wāthilah said, "I saw 'Alī ibn Abī Ṭālib speaking. I heard him say in his *khuṭbah*, 'Ask me. By Allah, you will not ask me about anything that will happen until the Day of Rising but that I will tell you about it. Ask me about the Book of Allah. By Allah, there is no *āyah* but that I know whether it was revealed at night or in the day, revealed on flat ground or on a mountain.'" Ibn al-Kawwā' rose and asked about Sūrat adh-Dhāriyāt (51).

"Abdullāh ibn Mas'ūd said, "If I knew of anyone with more knowledge of the Book of Allah than me, who could be reached by riding, I would go to him." A man asked him, "Have you not met 'Alī ibn Abī Ṭālib?" "Yes," he replied, "I have met him." Masrūq said, "I found some of the Companions of Muḥammad like pools which give water to one person, some like pools which give water to two, and some who are such that if all people came to it, it would satisfy their thirst. 'Abdullāh ibn Mas'ūd was one those pools."

'Abū Sa'īd al-Khudrī reported that the Messenger of Allah ﷺ said, "The most merciful to my community is Abū Bakr, the strongest in the *dīn* of Allah is 'Umar, the most truly modest is 'Uthmān, the one with the most knowledge of judgement is 'Alī, and the one with most knowledge of the shares of inheritance is Zayd. The one with the most recitation of the Book of Allah is Ubayy ibn Ka'b. The one with the most knowledge of the lawful and unlawful is Mu'ādh ibn Jabal. The trustworthy representative of this community is Abū 'Ubaydah ibn al-Jarrāḥ. Abū Hurayrah is a vessel of knowledge and Salmān is a sea of knowledge which is not perceived. Vegetation has not shaded nor has the earth supported anyone with a more truthful tongue than Abū Dharr."'

Ibn 'Aṭiyyah said, 'The prominent Followers (*Tābi'ūn*) included al-Ḥasan al-Baṣrī, Mujāhid, Sa'īd ibn Jubayr and 'Alqamah. Mujāhid studied recitation with Ibn 'Abbās, coupled with understanding the meaning, stopping at every *āyah*. 'Ikrimah and aḍ-Ḍaḥḥāk followed them. Even if aḍ-Ḍaḥḥāk did not meet Ibn 'Abbās, he studied with Ibn Jubayr. As for as-Suddī, 'Āmir ash-Sha'bī attacked him and Abū Ṣāliḥ because he thought that they fell short in careful investigation.'

Yaḥyā ibn Ma'īn said that al-Kalbī is nothing. Yaḥyā ibn Sa'īd al-Qaṭṭān related from Sufyān that al-Kalbī said that Abū Ṣāliḥ said, 'All that I have related to you is a lie.' Ḥabīb ibn Abī Thābit said, 'We used to call him "the Liar". He was Abū Ṣāliḥ, the freedman of Umm Hāni'.'

Then the *tafsīr* was transmitted by men of integrity of every generation. As the Prophet ﷺ said, 'This knowledge will be carried by men of integrity of every generation, discarding from it the deviation of the excessive, the ascriptions of the falsifiers and the interpretation of the ignorant.' Abū 'Umar and others related it. Al-Khaṭīb al-Baghdādī said, 'This testimony from the Messenger of Allah ﷺ shows that Qur'anic interpreters are scholars of the *dīn* and imams of the Muslims because they guard the Sharī'ah against deviation and the ascription of falsehood and refute the interpretation of ignorant fools. One must consult them and rely on them in the matter of the *dīn*.'

Ibn 'Aṭiyyah said, 'Then things were written about it by people like 'Abd ar-Razzāq, al-Mufaḍḍal, 'Alī ibn Abī Ṭalḥah, al-Bukhārī and others. Then Muḥammad ibn Jarīr collected disparate commentaries from people. He brought close that which was far and mended the *isnād*. The eminent later commentators include Abū Isḥāq az-Zajjāj and Abū 'Alī al-Fārisī. People often correct Abū Bakr an-Naqqāsh and Abū Ja'far an-Naḥḥās. Makkī ibn Abī Ṭālib followed their custom. Abu-l-'Abbās al-Mahdawī was a precise author. All of them strove and are rewarded. May Allah have mercy on them and illuminate their faces.'

The Book being explained by the Sunnah, and what has been transmitted about that

Allah says: '*And We have sent down the Reminder to you so that you can make clear to mankind what has been sent down to them*' (16:44), and: '*Those who oppose his command should beware of a testing trial coming to them or a painful punishment striking them*' (24:59) and: '*Truly you are guiding to a Straight Path.*' (42:49) The obligation of obeying the Prophet ﷺ is made clear in more than one *āyah* of Allah's Book and it is connected to obedience to Allah. Allah says: '*Whatever the Messenger gives you you should accept and whatever He forbids you you should forgo.*' (59:7) Ibn 'Abd al-Barr mentioned in the *Book of Knowledge* that 'Abd ar-Raḥmān ibn Yazīd saw a *muḥrim* wearing his ordinary clothes and he forbade him to do that. The man said to him, 'Bring me an *āyah* from the Book of Allah which removes my clothes.' He recited to him, '*Whatever the Messenger gives you you should accept and whatever He forbids you you should forgo.*' (59:7) Hishām ibn Ḥujayr said, 'Ṭāwūs prayed two *rak'ahs* after 'Aṣr and Ibn 'Abbās said, "Stop doing them." He answered, "It is only forbidden to take them as a sunnah." Ibn 'Abbās said, "The Messenger of Allah ﷺ forbade praying after 'Aṣr. I do not know whether you will be punished or rewarded for them, because Allah says, '*When Allah and His Messenger have decided a thing it is not for any believing man or believing woman to have a choice about it.*' (33:36)"'

Abū Dāwūd related from al-Miqdām ibn Ma'dikarīb that the Messenger of Allah ﷺ said, 'I was given the Book and its like along with it. It will not be long before a satiated man on his couch declares, "This Qur'an is all you need. Make lawful whatever you find lawful in it and make unlawful whatever you find unlawful in it." But domestic donkeys are not lawful for you, nor is eating any beast of prey with fangs, nor is something dropped by someone who has a treaty with you lawful to you, until its owner declares himself free of it. If someone stops with some people, they must give him hospitality. If they do not, he can legally pursue them for the equivalent cost of his due hospitality.'

Al-Khaṭṭābi said that the words 'I was given the Book and its like along with it' can be interpreted in two ways. One is that it means he was given hidden revelation, which is not recited, in the same way that he was given the outward recited part. The second is that he was given the Book as recited revelation and was given its equivalent in clarification of it, meaning permission to explain what was in the Book, making it general and specific, adding to it and legislating what is in it. Therefore it is as mandatory to act by that and to accept it as the outward recited Qur'an. This hadith is a warning against opposing those established sunnahs which are not in the Qur'an, as the Kharijites and Rafidites did. They attached themselves to the literal text of the Qur'an and abandoned those sunnahs which contain the clarification of the Book. Therefore they were confused and misguided. The word for 'couch' in the hadith is *'arīkah'*. It is only used for one with a curtained canopy and therefore it means the people of luxury and wealth who remain in their homes without bothering to seek for knowledge where it is expected to find it. This hadith contains evidence that there is no need to measure the hadith against the Book. Whatever is confirmed as being from the Prophet is evidence in itself. As for what some relate, 'When a hadith comes to you, measure it against the Book. If it agrees with it, take it. Otherwise, discard it,' it is a baseless false hadith.

This clarification is of two types: a general clarification of something undefined in the Book, like clarifying the five prayers, their times, prostration, *rukū'* and all their rulings, the amount and time of *zakāt* and the types of property from which it is taken, and the practices of ḥajj. When the Prophet ﷺ performed the ḥajj with the people, he said, 'Take your practices from me,' and he said, 'Pray as you saw me praying.' Al-Bukhārī transmitted it. 'Imrān ibn Ḥuṣayn said to a man, 'You stupid man! Do you find Ẓuhr in the Book of Allah as four *rak'ah*s in which recitation is not aloud!' Then he enumerated for him the prayer, *zakāt* and the like and then said, 'Do you find this explained in the Book of Allah? The Book of Allah Almighty did not define this; it is the Sunnah that explains it!'

Al-Awzā'ī reported that Ḥassān ibn 'Aṭiyyah said, 'Revelation descended on the Messenger of Allah ﷺ and Jibrīl brought him the Sunnah which explains it.' Sa'īd ibn Manṣūr related from 'Īsā ibn Yūnus from al-Awzā'ī and also reported that Makḥūl said, 'The Qur'an is more in need of the Sunnah than the Sunnah is of the Qur'an.' Yaḥyā ibn Abī Kathīr said, 'The Sunnah judges the Book and the Book does not judge the Sunnah.' Al-Fuḍayl ibn Ziyād said that he heard Aḥmad ibn Ḥanbal being asked about this hadith and he said, 'I am not so bold as to say that, but I do say that the Sunnah explains and clarifies the Book.'

Another area of clarification is augmentation of the rulings of the Book, like forbidding marrying a woman along with her maternal or paternal aunt, forbidding the consumption of domestic donkeys and every beast of prey with fangs, giving judgment based on an oath and a witness, and others as will be explained in the text, Allah willing.

How to learn and understand the Book of Allah and the Sunnah of His Prophet ﷺ, and what has been narrated about it being easier for someone who used to act by it without memorising it

In the *Kitāb al-Bayān*, Abū 'Amr ad-Dānī reports from 'Uthmān, Ibn Mas'ūd and Ubayy that the Messenger of Allah ﷺ used to recite ten *āyahs* to them, and they did not go on to another ten until they knew what action was connected to those *āyahs*. So we should learn the Qur'an and how to act by it at the same time. 'Abd ar-Razzāq mentioned from Ma'mar from 'Aṭā' ibn as-Sā'ib that 'Abd ar-Raḥmān as-Sulamī said, 'When we learned ten *āyahs* of the Qur'an, we did not learn the ten after them until we knew what they contained of the lawful and unlawful, of prohibitions and commands.' In the *Muwaṭṭā'*, Mālik reported that he heard that 'Abdullāh ibn 'Umar spent eight years learning Sūrat al-Baqarah. In his book, *The Names of Those who Transmitted from Mālik*, Abū Bakr Aḥmad ibn 'Alī ibn Thābit mentions from Abū Bilāl Mirdās ibn Muḥammad al-Ash'arī from Mālik that Nāfi' transmitted that Ibn 'Umar said, "Umar learned al-Baqarah over twelve years. When he finished, he slaughtered a camel.' Al-Anbārī reports from Muḥammad ibn Sharhiyār from Ḥusayn ibn al-Aswad from 'Ubaydullāh ibn Mūsā from Abū 'Amr Ziyād ibn Abī Muslim from Ziyād ibn Mikhrāq that 'Abdullāh ibn Mas'ūd said, 'It was difficult for us to memorise the words of the Qur'an, but easy for us to act by them. After us there will be people for whom it is easy to memorise the Qur'an, but hard to act by it.'

Ibrāhīm ibn Mūsā related from Yūsuf ibn Mūsā from al-Faḍl ibn Dukayn from Ismā'īl ibn Ibrāhīm ibn al-Muhājir from his father from Mujāhid that Ibn 'Umar said, 'The best of the Companions of the Messenger of Allah at the beginning of this Community only memorised a *sūrah* or two of the Qur'an. They were given the gift of acting by the Qur'an. The last of this community will recite the Qur'an – children and blind – and will not be given the gift of acting by it.' Abū Muḥammad Ḥasan ibn 'Abd al-Wahhāb ibn Abi-l-'Anbar from Abū Bakr ibn Ḥammād al-Muqrī' who heard Khalaf ibn Hishām al-Bazzār say, 'I only think that in our hands the Qur'an has been denuded [of action]. That is because we were told that 'Umar ibn al-Khaṭṭṭāb memorised Sūrat al-Baqarah over the course of about ten years. When he had memorised it, he slaughtered a camel to thank Allah. In our time, a boy sits before me and recites a third of the Qur'an without missing out a single letter. I only reckon that the Qur'an is denuded in our hands.'

Those with knowledge of hadith say that the person who seeks hadiths should not confine himself to listening to hadiths and reading their books without recognition and understanding. To do otherwise would mean tiring himself out with little result. His memorisation of hadiths should be undertaken gradually over nights and days. Among the masters of hadith from whom that is reported are Shu'bah, Ibn 'Ulayyah and Ma'mar. Ma'mar said that he heard az-Zuhrī say, 'Someone who seeks knowledge all at once loses out on all of it. Knowledge is acquired one or two hadiths at a time. Allah knows best.' Mu'ādh ibn Jabal said, 'Learn what you wish, but Allah will not reward you for it as long as you do not act on it.' Ibn 'Abd al-Barr said, 'Something similar to what Mu'ādh said is related from the Prophet ﷺ from 'Ubbād ibn 'Abd aṣ-Ṣamad which adds, 'The concern of scholars is comprehension and the concern of fools is mere transmission.' It is related *mawqūf* and is more fitting than the transmission which is *marfū'*. 'Ubbād ibn 'Abd aṣ-Ṣamad is not authoritative. There is an excellent poem on the excellence of knowledge and the honour of the Noble Book and Splendid Sunnah:

Even if the beauties of knowledge are majestic,
their crown is that in which belief is mandatory:
The Noble Book which Allah preserves.
After that is a knowledge that allays anxiety.
That is the hadiths of the Chosen, containing the light of Prophethood,
the Sunnah of Sharī'ah and good manners.
After this is knowledge without end.
So test yourself, you who prefer to seek.
Knowledge is a treasure which you will find in its mine.
Seeker! Study and look at books!
Recite the Book of Allah with understanding:
it contains all forms of knowledge. Reflect and you will see a marvel!
Read and you will be guided to the hadith of the Chosen.
Ask your Master for what you desire and your hope will be achieved.
Whoever tastes the knowledge of the *dīn* delights in it.
When he has more of it, he says, 'O joy!'

The meaning of the words of the Prophet ﷺ, "The Qur'an was revealed in seven *aḥruf* (dialects/modes)."

In *Ṣaḥīḥ Muslim*, Ubayy ibn Ka'b reported that the Prophet ﷺ was with the Banū Ghifār when Jibrīl came to him and said, 'Allah commands you to recite the Qur'an to your Community in one mode.' He said, 'I ask Allah for His pardon and forgiveness. My Community will not be able to do that.' Then he came a second time and said, 'Allah commands you to recite the Qur'an to your Community in two modes.' He said, 'I ask Allah for His pardon and forgiveness. My Community will not be able to do that.' He came a third time and said, 'Allah commands you to recite the Qur'an to your Community in three modes.' He replied, 'I ask Allah for His pardon and forgiveness. My Community will not be able to do that.' He came a fourth time and said, 'Allah commands you to recite the Qur'an to your community in seven modes. Whichever mode they recite, it is correct.' At-Tirmidhī reported that Ubayy said, 'The Messenger of Allah ﷺ met Jibrīl and said, "Jibrīl, I was sent to an illiterate community. Some of them are old women and old men, boys and girls, and men who do not read at all." He said to him, "Muḥammad, the Qur'an was revealed in seven modes."' He said that this is a sound hadith. This story is confirmed by the main authorities: al-Bukhārī, Muslim, the *Muwaṭṭā'*, Abū Dāwūd, an-Nasā'ī and other books in the form of the story about Hishām ibn Ḥakīm with 'Umar which we will mention later.

Scholars disagree about what is meant by the seven modes, and there are thirty-five things mentioned by Abū Ḥātim Muḥammad ibn Ḥibbān al-Bustī. We will mention five of them here:

This is the position of most of the people of knowledge, such as Sufyān ibn 'Uyaynah, 'Abdullāh ibn Wahb, aṭ-Ṭabarī, aṭ-Ṭaḥāwī and others. What is meant are the seven manners of synonyms with different expressions, like *aqbala, ta'āla* and *halumma* (all of which mean 'come here'). Aṭ-Ṭaḥāwī said, 'The clearest elucidation of that is what is mentioned in the hadith of Abū Bakrah, "Jibrīl came to the Prophet ﷺ and said, 'Recite in one mode.' Mīkā'īl said, 'Increase it.' He said, 'Recite it in two modes.' Mīkā'īl said, 'Increase it,' until it was seven modes. He said, 'Recite it. Each is adequate unless you confuse an *āyah* of mercy for an *āyah* of punishment or an *āyah* of punishment with an *āyah* of mercy.'" That is like *halumma, ta'āla, aqbala, adhhaba, asra'a* and *'ajjala.*' Warqā' related from Ibn Abī Najīḥ from Mujāhid from Ibn 'Abbās that Ubayy ibn Ka'b used to recite *'wait for us'* (57:13) *'undhurūnā'* as *'umhulūnā'*, *'akhkhirūnā'*, and *'arqubūnā'*. With the same *isnād*, it is reported that Ubayy recited in 2:19 *'marrū'* instead of '*mashaw*' and '*sa'aw*' (they walk). In al-Bukhārī, az-Zuhrī said, 'These modes are about the same matter. They do not differ in respect of the lawful and unlawful.'

Aṭ-Ṭaḥāwī said, 'There was allowance for people in respect of the letters since they were unable to take the Qur'an in other than their dialects because they were illiterate and only a few of them could write. It was hard for someone with a dialect to change to another. If he wanted to do that, it would have entailed great hardship and so they were given scope regarding different expressions as long as the meaning was the same. They remained like that until many of them could write and the dialects reverted to that of the Messenger of Allah ﷺ. Then they were able to memorise those words and they no longer had the allowance to recite differently.' Ibn 'Abd al-Barr said, 'It is clear that scope for the seven modes was at a particular time out of necessity. When that necessity was removed, the ruling of the seven was removed, and the Qur'an was recited in one mode.'

Abū Dāwūd related that Ubayy said, 'The Messenger of Allah ﷺ said to me, "Ubayy, I recited the Qur'an and was asked whether to recite it in one *ḥarf* or two. The angel who was with me told me to say, 'In two.' Then I was asked whether to recite it in two or three *ḥarf*s. The angel who was with me told me to say, 'In three.' This continued until it was seven." Then he said, "Any of these is comprehensive and sufficient. So you can say, '[Allah is] All-Hearing, All-Knowing, Almighty, and Wise,' as long as you do not muddle an *āyah* of punishment with mercy or an *āyah* of mercy with punishment."' Ibn Mas'ūd said something similar, Qāḍī Ibn aṭ-Ṭayyib said, 'If this transmission, namely the hadith of Ubayy, is confirmed, it can be assumed that it was general and then abrogated. Now it is not permitted for people to exchange the Names of Allah in different places whether or not that is in keeping with the meaning.'

Second view. Some people say that the seven dialects in the Qur'an are the seven dialects of all the Arabs, both Yemeni and Nizār, because the Messenger of Allah ﷺ was not ignorant of any of them. He was 'given concise comprehensive words'. It does not mean that the one mode has seven aspects, but these seven dialects are in different parts of the Qur'an. Some of it is in the dialect of Quraysh, some in that of Hudhayl, some in Hawāzin, and some in Yemeni.

Al-Khaṭṭābi said that there is in the Qur'an that which is recited in seven ways, which is His words, '*and who worshipped false gods?*' (5:60) and His words, '*Why don't you send him out with us tomorrow so he can enjoy himself and play about?*' (12:12) [both of which have variant readings], and he mentioned other examples, as if he took the position that some of the Qur'an was revealed in seven modes, not all of it.

The Qur'an being revealed in seven modes, i.e. in seven dialects was the position that Abū 'Ubayd al-Qāsim ibn Sallām took and Ibn 'Aṭiyyah preferred it. Abū 'Ubayd said, 'Some tribes have a greater share of it than others.' Ibn Shihāb mentioned from Anas that when 'Uthmān told them to copy out the Qur'an, he said, 'When you and Zayd differ, then write in the dialect of Quraysh. It was revealed in their dialect.' Al-Bukhārī mentioned it and he also mentioned what Ibn 'Abbās said: 'The Qur'an was revealed in the dialect of the two Ka'bs: Ka'b [ibn Lu'ayy] of Quraysh and Ka'b [ibn 'Amr] of Khuzā'ah.' He was asked, 'How is that?' He answered, 'Because they have the same abode.' Abū 'Ubayd said, 'It means that Khuzā'ah were the neighbours of Quraysh and so adopted their dialect.'

Qāḍī Ibn aṭ-Ṭayyib [al-Baqillānī] said, "Uthmān's words that it was revealed in the dialect of Quraysh means that most of it was revealed in that dialect. It is not a definitive proof that it is all in the dialect of Quraysh since there are words and letters which differ from the dialect of Quraysh. Allah says, '*We have made it an Arabic Qur'an.*' (43:3) He did not say, 'a Qurayshī Qur'an'. This indicates that it was revealed in the language of all the Arabs, and no one can say that it was just Quraysh or one part of the Arabs rather than others. So one cannot say that it means the dialect of 'Adnān rather than Qaḥṭān or Rabī'ah rather than Muḍar because the term 'Arab takes in all of these tribes.

Ibn 'Abd al-Barr said that he believed that saying that it was revealed in the dialect of Quraysh meant that most of it was revealed in the dialect of Quraysh because other dialects than that of Quraysh exist in sound readings with the use of the *hamzah*s and the like. Quraysh did not use the *hamzah*. Ibn 'Aṭiyyah said that the meaning of the 'seven modes' is that the expressions of all seven tribes are in it. It means that sometimes it is in the idiom of Quraysh, sometimes in the idiom of Hudhayl and sometimes in other idioms according to what is most eloquent and concise in expression. Do you not see that with Arabs other than Quraysh '*faṭr*' means beginning the creation of something and working on it? It comes in the Qur'an and Ibn 'Abbās was not directed to its meaning until two Bedouin came to him with a dispute over a well. One of them said, '*Anā faṭartuhā* (I began it).' Ibn 'Abbās said, 'Then I understood the meaning of the words of the Almighty: "*the Bringer into Being (Fāṭir) of the heavens and* *the earth.*" (6:14)' He also said, 'I did not know the meaning of His words, "*Our Lord, judge (iftaḥ) between us and our people with the truth.*" (7:89), until I heard the daughter of Dhū Yazin say to her husband, "Come and I will judge (*ufātiḥka*) you."' Similarly 'Umar ibn al-Khaṭṭāb said that he used to not understand the words of the Almighty, '*Or that He will no seize them little by little.*' (17:47) There are many examples of this.

Third view. The seven dialects are all from the tribes of Muḍar. Some people said that. They used as evidence what 'Uthmān said, 'The Qur'an was revealed in the language of Muḍar.' They said, 'It is possible that part of it is that of Quraysh, part Kinānah, part Asad, part Hudhayl, part Taym, part Ḍabbah, and part Qays.' They said these tribes of Muḍar contain the seven dialects in these ranks. Ibn Mas'ūd used to like those who copied out the Qur'ans to be from Muḍar. Others objected to the idea that it was all from Muḍar and said that there are rare usages in Muḍar with which it is not permitted to write the Qur'an.

What is related from some scholars is exemplified by Qāḍī Ibn aṭ-Ṭayyib who said, 'I have reflected on the aspects of the differences in recitation and have found them to be seven. Some involve changes of vowelling while the meaning and form remain, like "*aṭharu*" and "*aṭhara*" in 11:78; some do not change their form but change their meaning through inflection, as in 36:19, reading "*bā'id*" or "*bā'ada*"; some retain their form and change their meaning with different letters, like "*nunshizuhā*" (2:259) and "*nunshiruhā*"; some change the form while the meaning remains as in 101:5 where both '*ihn* and *ṣūf* mean wool; some change their form and meaning like "*ṭalḥin manḍūd*" (56:29) and "*ṭal'in manḍūd*"; some entail a change of order as in "*sakratu-l-mawt bi-l-ḥaqq*" and "*sakratu-l-ḥaqq bi-l-mawt*" in 50:19; and some consist of addition or reduction such as His words, "*ninety-nine* ***female*** *ewes*" (38:23), and "*As for the boy,* ***he was an unbeliever and*** *his parents were believers*" (18:80), "*then after they have been forced, Allah is Ever-Forgiving, Most Merciful* ***to them***" (24:33).

Fifth view. What is meant by the seven modes are meanings in the Book of Allah: command and prohibition, promise and threat, stories, arguments and parables. Ibn 'Aṭiyyah says that this is weak because that is not called *aḥruf*. Furthermore there is consensus that license is not granted in making the lawful lawful or changing any of the meanings. Qāḍī Ibn aṭ-Ṭayyib mentioned a hadith along these lines from the Prophet ﷺ and then said, 'This is not part of what it is allowed for them to recite. *Ḥarf* in this means 'manner' as Allah says, "*one who worships Allah on an edge.*" (22:11).' That is the meaning of this hadith about the seven means of allowing and forbidding and the like.

It is also said that what is meant by the seven *aḥruf* are the seven readings that we have because all of that is soundly transmitted from the Prophet ﷺ. This, however, is not correct, as we will now explain.

Section on the seven readings

Most scholars, like ad-Dāwūdī, Ibn Abī Ṣufrah and others said that these seven readings, which are ascribed to the seven readers, are not the seven *aḥruf* for which the Companions had an allowance to recite. They refer merely to one *ḥarf* of those seven, which is what 'Uthmān collected in the copy of the Qur'an which he authorised. Ibn an-Naḥḥās and others mentioned that. These seven famous readings (*qirā'āt*) are the selections of those Imams of recitation. That is because each of them chose what he related and the aspect he knew of the recitations that he considered to be the best and most appropriate. Each held to a path, related and recited it, and became famous for it. He is known for it and it is ascribed to him, like the mode of Nāfi' and the mode of Ibn Kathīr. None of them forbade choosing another nor objected to it. They allowed it. Each of those seven has two or more choices related from him. All are sound.

Muslims in this time have agreed to rely on what is soundly transmitted from these imams: that which they related of the readings and wrote in books. The consensus remains that they are correct and the preservation of the Book which Allah promised has been secured. This is the position of the earlier imams and excellent reliable men like Qāḍī Abū Bakr ibn aṭ-Ṭayyib, aṭ-Ṭabarī and others. Ibn 'Aṭiyyah said, 'These seven readings have lasted through different times and places and the prayer is performed using them, as their soundness is established by consensus. As for the rare (*shādhdh*) readings, the prayer is not performed using them because there is no consensus on doing that. As for what is related from the Companions and the *Tābi'ūn* about that, it can only be believed that they transmitted that. As for what is related from Abu-s-Sammāl and those connected to him, one does not rely on it.'

Someone else said, 'As for the rare (*shādhdh*) readings of the copies of the transmitted Qur'an, they are not considered to be the Qur'an, and are not acted on as if they were part of it. It is most probable that they are clarification of the interpretation of the position of the one to whom they are ascribed, like the reading of Ibn Mas'ūd. If the transmitter is explicit about having heard it from the Messenger of Allah ﷺ then scholars have two positions about acting on it: negative or positive. The negative position is based on the fact that the transmitter did not relate it as a hadith, but as Qur'an, and it is not affirmed as such and so is not confirmed. The positive position is that even if it is not affirmed as Qur'an, it is affirmed as sunnah, and that obliges action, just as the case with all single hadiths.'

Section: The hadith of 'Umar and Hishām

Ibn 'Aṭiyyah said, 'Allah allowed these seven modes to His Prophet ﷺ and Jibrīl brought them to him in a way which ensured inimitability and precise cohesion. His words, "*Recite what is easy of it*," did not permit any of the Companions to change any expression in one of these dialects as he wished. If that had been the case, then the Qur'an would not have been inimitable, as people would have changed this and that and then it would have become other than what was revealed from Allah. The permission was for the seven modes of the Prophet ﷺ in order to give ample scope to his Community. Once he recited to Ubayy what Jibrīl brought him, and once to Ibn Mas'ūd what had been presented to him.

'This was the crux of the difference between 'Umar ibn al-Khaṭṭāb's reading of Sūrat al-Furqān and that of Hishām ibn Ḥakīm. Otherwise how was it proper for the Prophet ﷺ to say about the recitation of each of them, which differed, "That was how Jibrīl recited it to me." Was it only that he recited it once like that and once like this? This is the meaning of what Anas said when he recited '*aṣwab*' instead of '*aqwam*' in Sūrat al-Muzzammil (73:5) meaning 'more conducive'. He was told, "We recite it '*aqwam*'." He replied, "'*Aṣwab*', '*aqwam*' and '*ahya'a*' are all the same." This is the sense of what is reported from the Prophet ﷺ. If anyone had been permitted to do that, that would have invalidated the words of Allah, "*It is We who have sent down the Reminder and We will preserve it.*" (15:9).'

Al-Bukhārī, Muslim and others related that 'Umar ibn al-Khaṭṭāb said, 'I heard Hishām ibn Ḥakīm reciting Sūrat al-Furqān in a different way from how I read it and how the Messenger of Allah ﷺ himself had recited it to me. I almost grabbed him but I waited until he had finished. Then I got him by his cloak and took him to the Messenger of Allah ﷺ. I said, "Messenger of Allah, I heard this one reciting Sūrat al-Furqān differently to how you recited it to me!" The Messenger of Allah ﷺ said, "Let him recite." He recited it as I had heard him recite it. The Messenger of Allah ﷺ said, "That is how it was revealed." Then he told me, "Recite." I recited it and he said, "That is how it was revealed. This Qur'an was revealed in seven modes, so recite whatever you find easy of it."'

Similar to this hadith is the one Muslim transmitted from Ubayy ibn Ka'b. He said, 'I was in the mosque when a man came in to pray. He recited a reading to which I objected. Then another man entered and recited a different recitation to that of his companion. When they finished the prayer, we all went to the Messenger of Allah ﷺ and I said, "This one recited a reading to which I objected and the other entered and used a different recitation to that of his companion." The Prophet ﷺ commanded them to recite, and the Prophet commended what they done. Then doubt entered my heart such as had not even affected me in the Jāhiliyyah. When the Prophet ﷺ saw what had overpowered me, he struck my chest and I started to sweat, feeling alarm as if I had been looking at Allah. He said to me, "Ubayy, I was sent a message to recite the Qur'an in one mode and I replied that I wanted it to be made easy for my community. A second message commanded me to recite it in two modes, and I replied that I wanted it to be made easy for my community. Then I was told the third time, 'Recite it in seven modes. You can ask for something for each time you returned to ask.' I said, 'O Allah, forgive my Community! O Allah, forgive my Community!' I delayed the third until a Day when all creation, even Ibrahim ﷺ will ask of me."'

Ubayy meant that he felt confusion and astonishment, in other words he had an impulse from Shayṭān which sullied his state and muddied his mind at that moment. The difference of the readings seemed terrible to him while it was not in itself terrible. Otherwise what would entail denial of the difference in the recitations, when that is not necessary? Praise be to Allah who abrogated what is greater than a reading! When the Prophet ﷺ saw the thought that occurred to him, he woke him up by striking his chest. The result of that was the expansion of his breast and inward illumination so that the unveiling and expansion took him to a state of vision. When the ugliness of that thought was clear to him, he feared Allah and sweated profusely out of shame before Allah. This thought is the type of thing about which the Prophet ﷺ spoke when they said to him, 'We find things in ourselves which one of us finds too terrible to speak about.' He asked, 'Do you experience that?' 'Yes,' they replied. He said, 'That is clear faith.' Muslim transmitted it from Abū Hurayrah. It will further be discussed in Sūrat al-A'rāf, Allah willing.

The collection of the Qur'an and the reason 'Uthmān had copies of the Qur'an copied out and burned the rest. The memorisation of the Qur'an by the Companions in the time of the Prophet ﷺ

In the time of the Prophet ﷺ, the Qur'an was scattered in the breasts of men. People wrote some of it in on pages, on skins and on white stones and flat stones, scraps and other things. Then a great number of reciters were killed in the Battle of Yamāmah in the time of Abū Bakr. Something like seven hundred of them were killed in a single day and 'Umar ibn al-Khaṭṭāb suggested to Abū Bakr that he should collect the Qur'an out of fear that the shaykhs of the reciters such as Ubayy, Ibn Mas'ūd and Zayd would all die. They deputised Zayd ibn Thābit to do that, and so after great effort, he collected it together without putting the *sūrahs* in order.

Al-Bukhārī reports that Zayd ibn Thābit said, 'After the slaughter in the war of Yamāmah, Abū Bakr sent for me, and 'Umar was with him. Abū Bakr said, "'Umar has come to me and said, 'Many people were killed in the Battle of Yamāmah, and I fear that many Qur'an reciters will be killed in other places and so much of the Qur'an will be lost unless you collect it together. I think that you should collect the Qur'an together.'" Abū Bakr said, "I said to 'Umar, 'How can I do something which the Messenger of Allah ﷺ did not do?' 'Umar said, 'By Allah, it is better.' 'Umar kept on at me about it until Allah opened my breast to it and I thought what 'Umar thought.'" Zayd ibn Thābit continued, "Umar was sitting with him, not speaking. Abū Bakr said, "You are an intelligent young man and we have no doubts about you. You used to write down the revelation for the Messenger of Allah ﷺ. Therefore, you are to search out the Qur'an and collect it." By Allah, if he had obliged me to move a mountain, that would not have been weightier for me than his command to me to collect together the Qur'an. I replied, "How can the two of you do something which the Messenger of Allah ﷺ did not do?" Abū Bakr said, "By Allah, it is better." He continued to keep on at me until Allah opened my breast to that to which Allah had opened the breasts of Abū Bakr and 'Umar. So I began to search out the Qur'an and collect it from the parchments, shoulder-blades, palm fronds and the breasts of men until I found two *āyahs* of Sūrat at-Tawbah with Khuzaymah al-Anṣārī that I did not find with anyone else: "*A Messenger has come to you from among yourselves...*" (9:128) The copy of the Qur'an in which the Qur'an was collected remained in the possession of Abū Bakr until Allah took him, and then it was with 'Umar until Allah took him, and then it was with Ḥafṣah bint 'Umar.'

Al-Layth related from 'Abd ar-Raḥmān ibn Ghālib that Ibn Shihāb said that it was with Abū Khuzaymah al-Anṣārī. Abū Thābit related that Ibrāhīm said that what was with Khuzaymah or Abū Khuzaymah was: *'But if they turn away, say, "Allah is enough for me. There is no god but Him. I have put my trust in Him. He is the Lord of the Mighty Throne."'* (9:129) At-Tirmidhī said in his hadith: 'I found the end of at-Tawbah with Khuzaymah ibn Thābit: *"A Messenger has come to you from among yourselves. Your suffering is distressing to him; he is deeply concerned for you; he is gentle and merciful to the believers But if they turn away, say, 'Allah is enough for me. There is no god but Him. I have put my trust in Him. He is the Lord of the Mighty Throne.' "* (9:128)' He said that it is a sound *ḥasan* hadith.

Al-Bukhārī related that Zayd ibn Thābit said, 'I missed one *āyah* of Sūrat al-Aḥzāb when we copied out the Qur'an which I used to hear the Messenger of Allah ﷺ recite. I only found it with Khuzaymah al-Anṣārī. It is that about which Zayd made the testimony of the Messenger of Allah ﷺ equal to that of two men: *"Men who have been true to the contract they made with Allah."* (33:23) At-Tirmidhī has: 'I missed one *āyah* of Sūrat al-Aḥzāb when we copied out the Qur'an which I used to hear the Messenger of Allah ﷺ recite: *"Among the believers are men who have been true to the contract they made with Allah."* I looked for it and found it with Khuzaymah ibn Thābit or Abū Khuzaymah and put it in its *sūrah*."

According to what al-Bukhārī and at-Tirmidhī said, the first *āyah* at the end of at-Tawbah was omitted from the first collection and the *āyah* from Sūrat al-Aḥzāb was omitted from the second. Aṭ-Ṭabarī said that the *āyah* from at-Tawbah was missing from the second collection. The first is sounder, and Allah knows best.

If it is asked what was the point of 'Uthmān unifying people under a single copy of the Qur'ān when Abū Bakr had already achieved that, then the response is that the aim of 'Uthmān was not to gather people in order to compile the Qur'an. Do you not see that he sent to Ḥafṣah to ask her to give him the copy of the Qur'an so that it could be copied out and then returned to her? 'Uthmān did that because people were disagreeing about the various recitations owing to the fact that the Companions had spread to different areas and had begun to strongly disagree, such as the conflict which took place between the people of Iraq and the people of Syria according to Ḥudhayfah.

They joined an expedition to Armenia and each group recited what had been transmitted to them. They disagreed and quarrelled and some of them called the others unbelievers, renouncing them completely, cursing one another. Ḥudhayfah was alarmed at what he saw. As soon as he arrived back in Madīnah, according to al-Bukhārī and at-Tirmidhī, before returning to his house he went to 'Uthmān and said, 'This Community has reached the stage where it will be destroyed!' 'Why?' asked 'Uthmān. He said, 'It is about the Book of Allah. I was on this expedition and some of the people of Iraq, Syria and the Hijaz came together.' Then he described what had happened and said, 'I fear that they will differ about their Book as the Jews and Christians differed.'

This is evidence of the falseness of those who say that the seven *aḥruf* are the seven present readings because there is no disagreement about them. Suwayd ibn Ghafalah reported from 'Alī ibn Abī Ṭālib that 'Uthmān said, 'What do you think about the copies of the Qur'an? The people have disagreed about the reciters until a man says, "My reading is better than your reading. My reading is more excellent than your reading." This is equivalent to disbelief.' He replied, 'What is your view, Amīr al-Mu'minīn?' He said, 'I think that we people should agree on one reading. If you differ today, those after you will disagree more strongly.' 'Alī said, 'The correct opinion is yours, Amīr al-Mu'minīn.' So 'Uthmān sent a message to Ḥafṣah saying, 'Send us the pages in your possession and we will copy them and then return them to you.' She sent them to him and he ordered Zayd ibn Thābit, 'Abdullāh ibn az-Zubayr, Sa'īd ibn al-'Āṣ, and 'Abd ar-Raḥmān ibn al-Ḥārith ibn Hishām to make copies of them. 'Uthmān told the group of Qurayshīs, 'When you and Zayd ibn Thābit disagree about any of the Qur'an, write it in the dialect of Quraysh. It was revealed in their language.' They did that. When they had copied it out, 'Uthmān returned the pages to Ḥafṣah and he sent a copy of what they had copied out to every region and commanded that every sheet or copy with any other form of the Qur'an in it should be burned. 'Uthmān did this after gathering the Muhājirūn and Anṣār and a group of Muslims and consulting them about it. They agreed to collect what was sound and firm of the well-known readings from the Prophet ﷺ and discard anything else. They thought that what he decided was right and correct. May Allah have mercy on him and all of them. Aṭ-Ṭabarī related that 'Uthmān brought together only Zayd and Abān ibn Sa'īd ibn al-'Āṣ. This is weak. What al-Bukhārī, at-Tirmidhī and others mentioned is sounder. Aṭ-Ṭabarī also said that the pages that Ḥafṣah had were the model for the final collection. This is sound.

Ibn Shihāb said that he was told by 'Ubaydullāh ibn 'Abdullāh that 'Abdullāh ibn Mas'ūd disliked Zayd ibn Thābit copying out the Qur'an and said, 'Company of Muslims, withdraw from making copies and entrusting it to one man. By Allah, I became Muslim while he was still in the loins of an unbelieving father!' meaning Zayd ibn Thābit. That is why 'Abdullāh ibn Mas'ūd said, 'People of Iraq, conceal the copies of the Qur'an you have and keep them concealed. Allah says, "*Those who misappropriate will arrive on the Day of Rising with what they have misappropriated.*" (3:161). Meet Allah with the copies of the Qur'an.' At-Tirmidhī transmitted it and it will be discussed in Āl 'Imrān, Allah willing.

Abū Bakr al-Anbārī said, 'The fact that Abū Bakr, 'Umar and 'Uthmān chose Zayd in the matter of collecting the Qur'an does not mean that they were putting him over 'Abdullāh ibn Mas'ūd. 'Abdullāh was better than Zayd, older in Islam, had attended more battles and possessed more virtues. Zayd, however, knew more of the Qur'an than 'Abdullāh since he had memorised it all during the lifetime of the Messenger of Allah ﷺ, whereas 'Abdullāh had only memorised about seventy *sūrah*s while the Messenger of Allah ﷺ was alive and learned the rest after his death. The one who knew the entire Qur'an and memorised it while the Messenger of Allah ﷺ was alive was more entitled to compile the Qur'an and to be preferred and chosen to do so. No ignorant person should suppose that this is an attack on 'Abdullāh ibn Mas'ūd since the fact that Zayd had the better memory of the Qur'an of the two does not mean that he should be preferred to him in general terms, because Zayd also knew more Qur'an than Abū Bakr and 'Umar, and he was certainly not better than them or equal to them in virtue.'

Abū Bakr al-Anbārī said, 'The objection which 'Abdullāh ibn Mas'ūd made was done in anger and is not acted upon or accepted. There is no doubt that once he was no longer angry he was satisfied with the excellence of the decision of 'Uthmān and the Companions of the Messenger of Allah ﷺ and concurred with their agreement and abandoned his opposition to them.'

It is commonly known among the people who study transmission that 'Abdullāh ibn Mas'ūd learned the rest of the Qur'an after the death of the Messenger of Allah ﷺ. One scholar said that 'Abdullāh ibn Mas'ūd died before learning all the Qur'an. Yazīd ibn Hārūn said, 'The two *sūrah*s of refuge have the same status as al-Baqarah and Āl 'Imrān. Anyone who claims that they are not part of the Qur'an has rejected Allah Almighty.' He was asked, 'What about what 'Abdullāh ibn Mas'ūd says about them?' He replied, 'There is no disagreement among the Muslims that

'Abdullāh ibn Mas'ūd died before memorising all of the Qur'an.' This requires some investigation, as will come later.

Ismā'īl ibn Isḥāq and others related that Ḥammād said – I think quoting Anas ibn Mālik – 'They disagreed about an *āyah* and would say, "The Messenger of Allah ﷺ recited it to so-and-so." He might be three days from Madīnah and he would be sent for and would be asked, "How did the Messenger of Allah ﷺ recite such-and-such an *āyah* to you?" and they would write it as he said.'

Ibn Shihāb said, 'One day they disagreed about *tābūt*. Zayd said *tābūh*. Ibn az-Zubayr and Sa'īd ibn al-'Āṣ said *tābūt*. The disagreement was taken to 'Uthmān who said, "Write it with *tā'*. It was revealed in the language of Quraysh."' Al-Bukhārī and at-Tirmidhī transmitted it. Ibn 'Aṭiyyah said, 'Zayd recited it with *hā'* and the Qurayshīs recited it with *tā'*. They confirmed it with *tā'* and the copies of the Qur'an have been written it as it was in the past. 'Uthmān had several copies of the Qur'an made. Some say there were seven while the majority say that there were four. They were sent to various areas. Matrix copies were sent to Iraq, Syria and Egypt, and the reciters of the cities relied on them and none of them differed from the original copy in the manner in which it was conveyed to them. No real difference in the wording is found among the seven reciters, neither more nor less. That is because they all relied on what was conveyed in 'Uthmān's copy since 'Uthmān wrote those places in some copies, but not others, which was a notification that it was sound and it was permitted to recite with all of them.

Ibn 'Aṭiyyah said, 'Then 'Uthmān commanded other copies to be burned or torn up (depending on whether that is read with a *ḥā'* as *tuḥraqu* (burned) or a *khā'* as *tukhraqu* (torn)). Then that was buried.' 'Burned' is a better transmission.

Abū Bakr al-Anbārī quoted Suwayd ibn Ghafalah in *Kitāb ar-Radd*, 'I heard 'Alī ibn Abī Ṭālib say, "Company of people! Fear Allah and beware of going to excess about 'Uthmān and calling him 'The burner of Qur'ans'. By Allah, he only burned them on the basis of the advice of a council of us, the Companions of Muḥammad ﷺ."' It is also reported from 'Umayr ibn Sa'īd that 'Alī ibn Abī Ṭālib said, 'If I had been ruler at the time of 'Uthmān, I would have done to the copies of the Qur'an the same thing that 'Uthmān did.'

Abu-l-Ḥasan ibn Baṭṭāl said, 'The fact that 'Uthmān ordered the parchments and copies of the Qur'an to be burned when the Qur'an was collected contains permission to burn writing which contains the

Names of Allah Almighty and shows that doing so is to honour it and protect it from being trodden on and thrown without care to the ground.' Ma'mar related from Ibn Ṭāwūs that his father used to burn pages when letters were collected with him that contained *'In the Name of Allah, the All-Merciful, Most Merciful.'* 'Urwah ibn az-Zubayr burned the books of *fiqh* he had at the time of the Battle of Ḥarrah. Ibrāhīm disliked burning pages when the name of Allah was on them. The position that they are burned is more likely to be correct. 'Uthmān did it. Qāḍī Abū Bakr said that it is permitted for the leader to burn papers which contain the Qur'an if he thinks that should be done.

Section

Our scholars say that what 'Uthmān did refutes the Ḥulūlīs (incarnationists) and Hashwites (anthropomorphists) who say that the letters and sounds are eternal and that recitation and reading are eternal and that faith is eternal and the *rūḥ* is eternal. The Community and all groups of the Christians, Jews and Brahmans believe – and indeed, so does every theist and unitarian – that that which is eternal is unaffected by any event and no one's power can affect it by any aspect or means. Non-existence is not possible for the eternal and the eternal does not become temporal and the temporal does not become eternal. As for the eternal, there is no beginning to its existence whereas the temporal is that which exists after it was not.

One group break the consensus of intelligent people of religions and others and say that it is permitted for the temporal to become eternal and that when the human servant of Allah recites the Words of Allah, the action of speaking the words of Allah is eternal. They say that it is the same when he carves letters from bricks and wood, or fashions letters from gold and silver, or weaves cloth on which he embroiders an *āyah* from the Book of Allah. Their action in doing that with the Words of Allah is eternal and so His words are woven and eternal, carved and eternal, and fashioned and eternal. They are told, 'In the case of what you say about the Words of Allah Almighty, can they be melted, effaced or burned?' If they answer affirmatively, then they have parted from the *dīn.* If they answer in the negative, they are told, 'So then what do say about the letters forming an *āyah* of the Book of Allah from wax, gold, silver, wood or paper which falls into a fire and melts or is burned? Do you say that the Words of Allah can be burned?' If they say, 'Yes,' then they have abandoned their position. If they say, 'No,' it is said to them,

'Did you not say that this writing is the Word of Allah? But it has been burned! Or these letters are His Word? But they have been melted!' If they then answer that it is the letters that have been burned while His Words remain, then they have returned to the truth and what is correct.

They are close to the answer that the Prophet ﷺ gave when calling attention to what the people of the truth say: 'If the Qur'an were in a skin and then fell into the fire, it would not burn.' Allah Almighty says, 'I sent down a Book to you which cannot be washed away by water and you recite it asleep and wake.' Muslim transmitted it. So it is confirmed that His Words are not letters and do not resemble letters. This is a topic which has been discussed at length and fully in the books of fundamental principles. We explained it in *Kitāb al-Asnā fī sharḥ asmā'i-llāhi-l-ḥusnā.*

Section

The Rafidites attack the Qur'an and say, 'One person is sufficient to confirm the transmission of an *āyah* and mode just as you have done. You confirmed the statement of a single man, Khuzaymah ibn Thābit, in reporting about the end of Sūrat at-Tawbah and the *āyah* in Sūrat al-Aḥzāb *"Among the believers are men…"* (33:23).' The reply to them is that when Khuzaymah mentioned these words, many of the Companions remembered them and Zayd himself recognised them. That is why he said, 'I missed the last two *āyah*s of Sūrat at-Tawbah.' If he had not already known them, he would not have known that something was missing. So the *āyah* was in fact established by consensus, not by Khuzaymah alone. A second answer is that it was established by the testimony of Khuzaymah alone and the evidence of its soundness is found in the description of the Prophet ﷺ and so has no need for another witness, which is not the case of the *āyah* in al-Aḥzāb. That is established by the testimony of Zayd and Abū Khuzaymah who both heard it from the Prophet ﷺ. Al-Muhallab said something similar and mentioned that Khuzaymah is not Abū Khuzaymah with whom the *āyah* of at-Tawbah was found and he was known among the Anṣār. Anas knew him and said, 'We inherited from him.' The one with whom the *āyah* of al-Aḥzāb was found was Khuzaymah ibn Thābit. There is no contradiction and it is not the same story. So there is no confusion about it.

Ibn 'Abd al-Barr said, 'Nothing is known about the name of Abū Khuzaymah. He is known by his *kunyah*, so he is Abū Khuzaymah ibn Aws ibn Zayd ibn Aṣram ibn Tha'labah ibn Ghunm ibn Mālik ibn an-Najjār. He was present at the Battle of Badr and the subsequent battles. He died while 'Uthmān ibn 'Affān was caliph. He was the brother of Mas'ūd ibn Aws.' Ibn Shihāb said that 'Ubayd ibn as-Sabbāq said that Zayd ibn Thābit said, 'I found the end of at-Tawbah with Abū Khuzaymah al-Anṣārī.' That is the case. There is no relationship between him and Abū Khuzaymah al-Ḥārith ibn Khuzaymah other than the fact they are both from the Anṣār. One was from Aws and the other from Khazraj.

In Muslim and al-Bukhārī, Anas ibn Mālik is reported as saying, 'The Qur'an was gathered together in the time of the Prophet ﷺ by four, all of whom were from the Anṣār: Ubayy, Mu'ādh ibn Jabal, Zayd ibn Thābit, and Abū Zayd.' Anas was asked, 'Who is Abū Zayd?' and he replied, 'One of my paternal uncles.' We also find in al-Bukhārī that Anas said, 'When the Prophet ﷺ died only four knew all the Qur'an: Abu-d-Dardā', Mu'ādh ibn Jabal, Zayd and Abū Zayd.' He said, 'We inherited from him.' In another transmission, he said, 'Abū Zayd died without leaving descendants. He had been present at Badr. The name of Abū Zayd was Sa'd ibn 'Ubayd.'

Ibn aṭ-Ṭayyib said, 'These traditions do not indicate that the Qur'an was not memorised in the time of the Prophet ﷺ and that only four of the Anṣār knew it by heart as Anas stated. It is confirmed by multiple paths of transmission that the entire Qur'an was also known by 'Uthmān, 'Alī, Tamīm ad-Dārī, 'Ubādah ibn aṣ-Ṣāmit, and 'Abdullāh ibn 'Amr ibn al-'Āṣ. Anas' words mean that only these four took it directly from the mouth of the Messenger of Allah ﷺ. Most of them learned some of it from him and some of it from others. The transmissions corroborate each other about the four imams knowing all the Qur'an during the lifetime of the Prophet ﷺ due to the fact that they became Muslim early on and the Messenger ﷺ held them in great esteem.'

The Qāḍī did not mention 'Abdullāh ibn Mas'ūd and Sālim, the client of Abū Ḥudhayfah, although they were among those who knew the entire Qur'an. Jarīr related from 'Abdullāh ibn Yazīd aṣ-Ṣuhbānī from Kumayl that 'Umar ibn al-Khaṭṭāb said, 'I was with the Messenger of Allah ﷺ and with him were Abū Bakr and whomever Allah wished. We passed 'Abdullāh ibn Mas'ūd who was praying. The Messenger of Allah ﷺ asked, "Who is reciting the Qur'an?" He was told, "'Abdullāh ibn Umm 'Abd" He said, "'Abdullāh recites the Qur'an fresh as it was revealed."'

One scholar said that this meant that he recited the first *ḥarf* in which the Qur'an was revealed rather than the other seven, which the Messenger of Allah ﷺ was allowed after the Messenger of Allah, Jibrīl, recited the Qur'an to him in Ramadan. It is related that Abū Ẓubyān said, "Abdullāh ibn 'Abbās asked me, "Which of the recitations do you recite?" I replied, "The first recitation, that of Ibn Umm 'Abd." He told me, "Rather it was the last. The Messenger of Allah ﷺ used to present the Qur'an to Jibrīl once a year. In the year that he died, the Messenger of Allah ﷺ recited it to him twice. 'Abdullāh was present and knew what was abrogated and changed in that recitation."' In Muslim, 'Abdullāh ibn 'Amr stated that he heard the Messenger of Allah ﷺ say, 'Take the Qur'an from four: Ibn Umm 'Abd – and he began with him – Mu'ādh ibn Jabal, Ubayy ibn Ka'b and Sālim, the client of Abū Ḥudhayfah.'

These reports indicate that 'Abdullāh knew all the Qur'an in the lifetime of the Messenger of Allah ﷺ, contrary to what was said, and Allah knows best. In *Kitāb ar-Radd*, Abū Bakr al-Anbārī transmitted that 'Abdullāh ibn Mas'ūd said, 'I learned 72 (or 73) *sūrahs* from the Messenger of Allah ﷺ and I read to him from al-Baqarah as far as "*Allah loves those who repent*" (2:222).' Abū Isḥāq says that he learned the rest of the Qur'an from Mujammi' ibn Jāriyah al-Anṣārī. If this is true, the consensus which Yazīd ibn Hārūn mentioned is true and that is why Qāḍī Ibn aṭ-Ṭayyib did not mention him among those who knew the Qur'an by heart in the time of the Messenger of Allah ﷺ. Allah knows best.

Abū Bakr al-Anbārī related from Ibrāhīm ibn Mūsā al-Khūdrī from Yūsuf ibn Mūsā from Mālik ibn Ismā'īl from Zuhayr that Abū Isḥāq said, 'I asked al-Aswad what 'Abdullāh used to do with respect to Sūrat al-A'rāf. He said, "He did not know it until he came to Kufa."' He said that one of the people of knowledge said, "Abdullāh ibn Mas'ūd died before he learned the two *sūrahs* of Refuge. That is why they were not found in his copy of the Qur'an.' Other things are said which will be dealt with at the end of the book, Allah willing.

Abū Bakr said that Ibrāhīm ibn Mūsā related from Yūsuf ibn Mūsā from 'Umar ibn Hārūn al-Khurāsānī from Rabī'ah ibn 'Uthmān that Muḥammad ibn Ka'b al-Quraẓī said, 'Among those who knew the Qur'an by heart when the Messenger of Allah ﷺ was alive were 'Uthmān ibn 'Affān, 'Alī ibn Abī Ṭālib and 'Abdullāh ibn Mas'ūd.' The people of knowledge do not consider the hadith to be sound. It stops at Muḥammad ibn Ka'b and so it is severed. It is not taken nor relied on.

The words of the Prophet ﷺ, 'Take the Qur'an from four: Ibn Umm 'Abd...' indicate its soundness. Part of what will make that clear is that the people with the readings among the people of the Hijaz, Syria and Iraq all traced their readings which they chose back to one of the Companions who read it to the Messenger of Allah ﷺ and did not exclude anything from the entire Qur'an. 'Āṣim traced his reading to 'Alī and Ibn Mas'ūd, Ibn Kathīr to Ubayy as did Abū 'Amr ibn al-'Alā', and 'Abdullāh ibn 'Āmir traced his to 'Uthmān. All of them said that they had read it to the Messenger of Allah ﷺ. The *isnād*s of these readings are continuous and the transmitters are reliable, as al-Khaṭṭābī stated.

What has come about the order of the *sūrah*s and *āyah*s of the Qur'an, its vowelling and dots, its *ḥizb*s and tens, the number of its letters, *juz'*s, words and *āyah*s

Ibn aṭ-Ṭayyib said, 'Some say that the Salaf differed about the order of the *sūrahs* of the Qur'an and some of them wrote the *sūrah*s in the order that they were revealed and put the Makkan before the Madinan, and some put al-Ḥamd (Fātiḥah) at the beginning, and others put al-'Alaq at the beginning. This was the case in the first copy of 'Alī. As for the copy of Ibn Mas'ūd, it begins with "*Master of the Day of the Dīn*" (1:4) and then al-Baqarah, and then an-Nisā' with a different order. The copy of Ubayy began with al-Ḥamd, then an-Nisā', then Āl 'Imrān, then al-An'ām, then al-A'rāf, then al-Mā'idah. There were significant differences.'

The answer of Qāḍī Abū Bakr ibn aṭ-Ṭayyib is that it is possible that the order of the *sūrah*s we have today in the Qur'an is by *ijtihād* on the part of the Companions. Makkī mentioned this in the *tafsīr* of Surat at-Tawbah. He mentioned the order of the *āyah*s in the *sūrah* and that placing the *basmalah* at the beginnings of them was from the Prophet ﷺ. Since he did not command that for Sūrat at-Tawbah, it was left without a *basmalah*. This is the soundest of what is said about it.

In the *Jāmi'*, Ibn Wahb stated that Sulaymān ibn Bilāl heard Rabī'ah being asked why al-Baqarah and Āl 'Imrān were put first when there were about eighty *sūrah*s revealed before them and they were revealed in Madīnah. Rabī'ah said, 'They were put first and the Qur'an was arranged according to the knowledge of those who arranged it and had knowledge of that. This is what we ended up with and we do not ask about it.' Sunayd mentioned from Mu'tamir from Sallām ibn Miskīn from Qatādah that Ibn Mas'ūd said, 'Whoever of you seeks a model, should model himself on the Companions of the Messenger of Allah ﷺ. They have the best hearts of this community, the deepest knowledge, least artifice, straightest guidance and the best state. Allah chose them to be the Companions of His Prophet ﷺ and to establish His *dīn*. So acknowledge their excellence and follow in their footsteps. They followed straight guidance.'

Some scholars say that the arrangement of the *sūrahs* of the Qur'an which we find in our copies of the Qur'an was at the instruction of the Prophet ﷺ. What is related about the differences between the copies of Ubayy, 'Alī and 'Abdullāh was before the final presentation. The Messenger of Allah ﷺ arranged those *sūrahs* for them after they had done that. Yūnus related from Ibn Wahb that he heard Mālik say, 'The Qur'an was arranged according to what they heard from the Messenger of Allah ﷺ.'

Abū Bakr al-Anbārī mentioned in *Kitāb ar-Radd*, 'Allah Almighty revealed the Qur'an all at once to the lowest heaven, and then it came down in parts to the Prophet ﷺ over twenty years. A *sūrah* would be revealed about a matter which happened and an *āyah* would answer an inquiry. Jibrīl would give the Messenger of Allah ﷺ the place of the *sūrah* and the *āyah*. So the *sūrahs* are in order as the *āyahs* and letters are in order. All of it is from Muḥammad, the Seal of the Messengers ﷺ from the Lord of the Worlds. Whoever changes the order of the *sūrahs* is like someone who nullifies the order of the *āyahs* and changes the letters and the words. There is no argument against the people who possess the truth in putting al-Baqarah before al-An'ām when al-An'ām was revealed before al-Baqarah because the order is taken from the Messenger of Allah ﷺ. He said, "Put this *sūrah* in such-and-such a place in the Qur'an." Jibrīl acquainted him with the position of the *āyahs*.'

Ḥasan ibn al-Ḥubāb related from Abū Bakr ibn 'Ayyāsh from Abū Isḥāq that al-Barā' said, 'The last of the Qur'an to be revealed was, "*They will ask you for a fatwā. Say: 'Allah gives you a fatwā about people who die without direct heirs.'*" (4:175).' Abū Bakr ibn 'Ayyāsh said, 'Abū Isḥāq erred because it is reported from Ibn 'Abbās that the last part of the Qur'an to be revealed was, "*Show fear of a Day when you will be returned to Allah. Then every self will be paid in full for what it earned. They will not be wronged*" (2:281). Jibrīl told the Prophet ﷺ, "Muḥammad, put it at the beginning of *āyah* 281 of al-Baqarah."'

Abu-l-Ḥasan ibn Baṭṭāl said, 'Whoever says this, does not say that the recitation of the Qur'an in the prayer and lessons must be in the order that it is in copies of the Qur'an. Rather it is only mandatory to put the *sūrahs* in order when writing them down, and it is not known that any of them said that the same order is mandatory in the prayer or in recitation of the Qur'an and study, or that it is not lawful for someone to learn al-Kahf before al-Baqarah or al-Ḥajj before al-Kahf. Do you not see that 'Ā'ishah told the person who asked about this, "There is nothing wrong in whichever you recite first. The Prophet ﷺ used to recite one *sūrah* in a *rak'ah* and then would recite in the next *rak'ah* a different *sūrah* than the one that follows it."

'As for what is reported from Ibn Mas'ūd and Ibn 'Umar about it being disliked to recite the Qur'an out of order, claiming that it upsets the heart, what they meant by that was reciting the *sūrah* out of order and beginning from its end and then working backwards, because that is forbidden. Some people do this with the Qur'an and poetry to subject the tongue to that and facilitate memorisation. Allah forbade doing this in the Qur'an because it disorders His *sūrah*s and is counter to what He meant by it.'

Part of what indicates that it is not mandatory to use the chronological order of revelation in copies of the Qur'an is that it is confirmed that certain *āyah*s were revealed in Madīnah and then placed in Makkan *sūrah*s. 'Ā'ishah said, "Sūrat al-Baqarah and Sūrat an-Nisā' were revealed when I was with him (i.e. in Madīnah) but they come in the copies of the Qur'an before earlier *sūrah*s of the Qur'an revealed in Makkah." If they had been arranged by historical revelation, it would be obliged to break the order of the *āyah*s of the *sūrah*s.

Abū Bakr al-Anbārī related from Qāḍī Ismā'īl ibn Isḥāq from Ḥajjāj ibn Minhāl from Hishām that Qatādah said, 'The *sūrah*s of the Qur'an revealed in Madīnah were: al-Baqarah, Āl 'Imrān, an-Nisā', al-Mā'idah, al-Anfāl, at-Tawbah, ar-Ra'd, an-Naḥl, al-Ḥajj, an-Nūr, al-Aḥzāb, Muḥammad, al-Fatḥ, al-Ḥujurāt, ar-Raḥmān, al-Ḥadīd, al-Mujādalah, al-Mumtaḥanah, aṣ-Ṣaff, al-Jumu'ah, al-Munāfiqūn, at-Taghābun, aṭ-Ṭalāq, at-Taḥrīm, az-Zilzāl, and an-Naṣr. Those *sūrah*s were revealed in Madīnah while the rest were revealed in Makkah.'

Abū Bakr said, 'If someone abandons traditions, turns away from consensus and orders the *sūrah*s based on their positions in Madīnah and Makkah, he does not know where to put the Fātiḥah, because of people's disagreement about where it was revealed, and needs to delay the *āyah* at the beginning of 235 of al-Baqarah to the beginning of 240. If someone ruins the order of the Qur'an, he has disbelieved in it and rejects what Muḥammad ﷺ related from his Lord. It is said the reason for putting the Madinan before the Makkan is that Allah Almighty addressed the Arabs in their language, using the styles of speech and discourse that they knew. When one of their linguistic styles was based on alteration of the order in speech, they were addressed in that way in the Book of Allah Almighty. Had they noticed it missing from the Qur'an, they would asked why this was missing from it.'

Section

As for the diacritical marks of the Qur'an and its dots, it is reported that 'Abd al-Malik ibn Marwān commanded them to be added, and that was undertaken by al-Ḥajjāj in Wasit. He worked on the task and added its *ḥizb*s. He commanded the governor of Iraq, al-Ḥasan, and Yaḥyā ibn Ya'mar to do that. After that he wrote a book in Wasit on the readings, in which he compiled what was related about the disagreement of people in relation to the script. People used that book for a long time until Ibn Mujāhid wrote his book on the readings. In *Kitāb aṭ-Ṭabaqāt* az-Zubaydī quotes al-Mubarrad as saying that the first person to use dots in the Qur'an was Abu-l-Aswad ad-Du'alī. Ibn Sīrīn also mentioned that he had a copy of the Qur'an in which Yaḥyā ibn Ya'mar had put the dots.

Section

As for the position regarding the division of the Qur'an into groups of ten *āyah* or *a'shār*, Ibn 'Aṭiyyah said, 'In one of the histories I read that the Abbasid al-Ma'mūn commanded that to be done. It is also said that al-Ḥajjāj did it.' In the *Kitāb al-Bayān*, ad-Dānī said that 'Abdullāh ibn Mas'ūd disliked the marking of tens in the copies of the Qur'an and that he erased them. Mujāhid is reported to have disliked the signs for tens in copies of the Qur'an.

Ashhab said, 'I heard Mālik being asked about the signs for tens which are in the Qur'an in red and other colours and he disliked that, saying, "There is nothing wrong in marking the tens with [normal] ink." He was asked about copies of the Qur'an in which the ends of *sūrah*s were written along with the number of *āyah*s in every *sūrah*. He said, "I dislike anything [additional] being written or vowelled in the master copies. As for those copies by which children learn, I see no harm in doing that."' Ashhab said, 'Then he produced for us a copy of the Qur'an which had belonged to his grandfather. He had written it when 'Uthmān had the Qur'an copied out. We saw the ends were written in ink in something resembling a chain which extended for an entire line and I saw that the *āyah*s had diacritical marks in ink.'

Qatādah said, 'They began with the dots, then with marking the division of the fives and then the tens.' Yaḥyā ibn Abī Kathīr said, 'The Qur'an was bare in the original copies and the first thing that they did was to put dots on the *bā'*, *tā'* and *thā'*. They said, "There is nothing wrong in it. It makes it clearer." Then they put dots at the ends of *āyah*s and then they put openings and ends of *sūrah*s.'

Abū Ḥamzah said, 'Ibrāhīm an-Nakha'ī noticed in my copy of the Qur'an the opening of such-and-such a *sūrah*. He said to me, "Erase it. 'Abdullāh ibn Mas'ūd said, 'Do not mix with the Book of Allah something which is not part of it.'"' Abū Bakr as-Sarrāj said, 'I asked Abū Rāzin, "Do I write Sūrah such-and-such in my copy of the Qur'an?" He replied, "I fear that people will come who do not know it and think that those words are part of the Qur'an."'

Ad-Dānī said, 'All these reports which allow the marking of tens and fives and beginnings of *sūrah*s and the beginnings of *āyah*s say that it was done by the Companions whose *ijtihād* led them to that. I think that those of them who objected to that objected to the use of colours like red, yellow and so forth, although the Muslims in other areas agreed on their use in the master copies and other copies, and prohibition and error were removed from them in what they agreed upon, Allah willing.'

Section

As for the number of its letters and *juz'*s, Sallām al-Ḥimānī said, 'Al-Ḥajjāj ibn Yūsuf gathered the reciters, *ḥuffāẓ* and scribes and said, "Tell me how many letters there are in the entire Qur'an." I was one of that group. We calculated and agreed that the Qur'an had three hundred and forty thousand, seven hundred and forty (340, 740) letters. Then he said, "Tell me which letter ends half of the Qur'an." It was in al-Kahf, on the *fā'* of *wa-l-yatalaṭṭaf* [18:19, "*he should go about with caution.*"]" He said, "Tell me the thirds." The first third was found to be at the beginning of 9:100 and at the second at the beginning of 26:100 or 101. The last third was the rest of the Qur'an. He said, "Tell me the sevenths of the letters." The first seventh was on the *dāl* in 4:55, the second on the *tā'* in 9:77, the third on the *alif* in 11:35, the fourth on the *alif* in 22:34, the fifth on the *hā'* in 33:36, the sixth on the *wāw* in 48:6, and the seventh consists of the rest of the Qur'an.'

Abū Muḥammad Sallām stated, 'We did that over four months. Every night al-Ḥajjāj would read a fourth. The end of the first fourth was at the end of al-An'ām, the second in al-Kahf, the third at the end of az-Zumar and the fourth consisted of the rest.' This is contrary to what is mentioned by ad-Dānī in *Kitāb al-Bayān*.

Section

As for the number of the *āyah*s of the Qur'an in the first Madinan copy, Muḥammad ibn 'Īsā said, 'The number of the *āyah*s of the Qur'an in the first Madinan copy was six thousand.' Abū 'Amr said, 'It is the number related by the people of Kufa from the people of Madīnah, and they did not name anyone specifically on whom they relied in that.'

As for the final Madinan copy, according to Ismā'īl ibn Ja'far, it has six thousand two hundred and fourteen (6214) *āyahs*. Al-Faḍl said, 'The number of the *āyahs* of the Qur'an according to the Makkans was six thousand two hundred and nineteen (6219). That is the number related by Sālim and al-Kisā'ī from Ḥamzah. Al-Kisā'ī attributed it to 'Alī.' Muḥammad said, 'The number of the *āyahs* of the Qur'an according to the Basrans was six thousand two hundred and four (6204), which is the number which their Salaf passed down. As for the number of the people of Syria, Yaḥyā ibn al-Ḥārith adh-Dhimārī said it was six thousand two hundred and twenty-six (6226). One transmission has six thousand two hundred and twenty-five (6225).' Ibn Dhakwān said, 'I think that Yaḥyā did not count the *basmalah*.' Abū 'Amr said, 'These are the numbers that people have exchanged and counted in all regions, in the past and recently.'

As for the number of its words, al-Faḍl ibn Shādhān said, 'The total number of the words of the Qur'an according to 'Aṭā' ibn Yasār is seventy-seven thousand four hundred and thirty-nine (77,439) and its letters are three hundred and twenty-three thousand, and fifteen (323,015).' This differs from what al-Ḥimānī said. Ibn Kathīr reported that Mujāhid said, 'This is what we counted of the Qur'an: it has three hundred and twenty-one thousand, one hundred and eighty (321,180) letters.' This also differs from what al-Ḥimānī mentioned.

The meaning of the words *sūrah, āyah, kalimah* (word) and *ḥarf* (letter)

The word '*sūrah*', which means chapter, wall or fence in Arabic, is used in the Qur'an to make each chapter clear and distinct from every other *sūrah*. The chapters are called that because in them one ascends from one degree to the next. It is said that they are called that because of their honour and elevation, as is said of walls which are raised up in the land. It is said that they are called that because the one who reads them looks forward at what lies ahead, like the walls of a building. All these are without *hamzah*. It is said that they are called that because they are cut out from the Qur'an on their own, as the Arabs call a leftover *su'r*. In that case the word would have a *hamzah* which was replaced with a *wāw*. It is said that they are called that because of their completion and perfection as this word is used for a fine camel.

An *āyah* is a sign. It is a sign since it is separate and distinct from the words before it and the words after it; it is clear from other signs and is on its own. The Arabs say, 'There is an *āyah* between me and so-and-so,' meaning a sign. That is also its usage in: '*The sign of his kingship.*' (2:248) It is said that it is called that because it is a collection of letters of the Qur'an, as one says, 'The people went forth with their full company (*āyah*).' It is said that it is called *āyah* because it is a wonder which people are unable to imitate.

Grammarians disagree about the root of *āyah*. Sībawayh said that it is *ayayah* on the measure of *fa'alah* and because the *yā'* is vowelled and has a *fatḥah* before it, it becomes *alif* and so it is *āyah*. Al-Kisā'ī said that its root is *ayayah* and the *yā'* accepts the *alif* with a *fatḥah* before it and is elided because they are similar. Al-Farrā' says that its root is *ayyayah* and it accepts the *alif* out of dislike of the doubling and becomes *āyah*.

As for word (*kalimah*), it is a composite structure which is made up of a mixture of letters. The longest words in the Book of Allah are eleven letters long, like "*la-yastakhlifannahum*" (24:55) and "*a-nulzimukumūhā*" (11:28) and the like. As for "*fa-asqaynakumūhu*" (15:22), it is ten in writing and eleven in articulation. The shortest have two letters, like *mā, la, laka, lahu*, and the like. Some words are just one letter, such as the interrogative *hamzah* and the conjunctive *wāw*, but are not enunciated on their own.

Sometimes a complete *āyah* is comprised of a single word, as in *wa-l-fajr, wa-ḍ-duḥā*, and *wa-l-'aṣr*. That is also the case in *alif-lām-mīm, alif-lām-mīm-ṣād, ṭā-hā, yā-sīn*, and *ḥā-mīm* according to the Kufans. That occurs at the beginnings of *sūrah*s, but not inside them. Abū 'Amr ad-Dānī said, 'I do not know of any word which on its own is an *āyah* except for *mudhāmmatān* in Sūrat ar-Raḥmān (55:64).' Two words may become connected and be two *āyah*s, as in *ḥā-mīm 'ayn-sīn-qāf* according to the Kufans.

It is possible that elsewhere a single word may stand for a complete and self-sustaining *āyah*. Allah says: '*The most excellent Word of your Lord was fulfilled for the Tribe of Israel for their steadfastness.*' (7:136-137) It is said that 'word' here refers to Allah's words: '*We desired to show kindness to those who were oppressed in the land.*' (28:4-5) The Almighty says, '*He bound them to godfearing self-restraint* (literally '*word of taqwā*')' (48:26). Mujāhid said that the 'word' is: 'There is no god but Allah.' The Prophet ﷺ said, 'Two words are light on the tongue, heavy in the balance, beloved to the All-Merciful: "Glory be to Allah and by His praise. Glory be to Allah, the Immense."' The Arabs sometimes call an entire ode and story a 'word' since it is their custom to call a thing by the name of what it comes from or is close to it and it is metaphorical.

The word *ḥarf* (letter) is the shape which stands alone in a word of which it is made up. A letter can be called a word and a word a letter as we made clear. Abū 'Amr ad-Dānī said, 'Are the letters of the alphabet at the beginnings of *sūrahs*, such as *ṣād, qāf,* and *nūn* letters or words? I say that they are words, not letters. That is because a letter is not unvowelled nor is it alone in a *sūrah* nor separate from what is mixed with it. But these are unvowelled, alone, separate, like words which are distinct. That is why they are called words rather than letters.' Abū 'Amr said that the term '*ḥarf*' can also be used with the meaning of a direction as in 22:11. Similarly the *aḥruf* of the Qur'an are seven modes of language. Allah knows best.'

Does the Qur'an contain words which are not Arabic?

There is no disagreement among the imams that the Qur'an contains words composed in a non-Arabic mode and names of people which are not Arabic, such as Isrā'īl, Jibrīl, 'Imrān, Nūḥ and Lūṭ. They disagree about whether there are words other than proper names that are non-Arabic. Qāḍī Ibn aṭ-Ṭayyib, aṭ-Ṭabarī and others believe that there are no non-Arabic words in it and the Qur'an is pure Arabic, and whatever words found in it ascribed to other languages happen to be common to both, and so the Arabs, Persians, Abyssinians and others used them. Some claim that non-Arabic words exist in the Qur'an but that since they are so few that does not preclude the Qur'an being pure Arabic and the Prophet ﷺ from speaking the language of his people. *Mishkāt* (24:35) is a niche, *nasha'a* means 'to rise in the night' as in '*nāshi'ata-l-layl*' (73:6), *qaswarah* (74:51) is a lion and *kiflayn* (57:28) means 'double'. These are found in Abyssinian. *Ghassāq* (38:57) means 'foul' in Turkish. *Qisṭās* (17:35; 26:182) means 'balance' in Greek. *Sijjīl* (21:104; 15:74; 105:4) means 'stones' in Persian. *Ṭūr* (2:63; 2:93, etc.) is a mountain and *yamm* (7:136. etc.) means sea in Syriac. *Tannūr* (11:40; 23:27) is the surface of the earth in Persian.

Ibn 'Aṭiyyah said, 'The truth about the expression of these words is that their origin is foreign but the Arabs used them and Arabicised them and so they are Arabic. When the Qur'an was revealed in their language, the Arabs had mixed with other languages via trade and travel. There were the journeys of Quraysh and the journey of Musāfir ibn Abī 'Amr to Syria, the journeys of 'Umar ibn al-Khaṭṭāb, 'Amr ibn al-'Āṣ and

'Ammārah ibn al-Walīd to Abyssinia, and the journeys of al-A'shā to Hira [in Iraq] and his keeping the company of the Christians there: he is considered to be an authority in language. Through all of that the Arabs acquired foreign words and changed some of them by reducing the number of letters and lessening their foreign quality. They used them in their poetry and conversations until they became part of sound Arabic and are clear. It is according to this that the Qur'an was revealed. If an Arab is ignorant of it, it is clear ignorance of another language, just as Ibn 'Abbās did not know the meaning of '*fāṭir*' and other things.' Ibn 'Aṭiyyah said, 'What aṭ-Ṭabarī believed about the two languages both using the same expressions is unlikely. Rather one of them is the root and the other the branch in most cases.'

Others say that the first is sounder. The statement that the root of the words come from another language and have entered Arabic is not more appropriate than the reverse. The Arabs either spoke them or did not. If the first is true, then it is part of their language. It is not unlikely for others to use the same words. The great imam Abū 'Ubayd said that.

If it is said that the words do not have the morphological forms of Arabic words and so they are not from Arabic, we say that if someone tells you that their morphological forms are limited so that these words are not part of them, the Qāḍī has investigated the bases of the morphological forms of Arabic and returned these words to them by a grammatical approach. If the Arabs did not speak them or know them, it would be impossible for Allah to address them by something they did not know. In that case, the Arabic would not be clear Arabic and the Messenger ﷺ would not be addressing his people in their language. And Allah knows best.

Points about the inimitability of the Qur'an, preconditions of the miracle and its reality

A miracle (*mu'jizah*) is the proof of the Prophets which indicates their truthfulness. It is called that [the verb means 'to be unable to do'] because no human being is able to do the like of it. It has five preconditions. If one of them is missing, it is not a miracle.

– It must be something which only Allah can do. This precondition is necessary because if someone comes at a time in which it is possible for there to be Messengers and claims to be a Messenger and makes his miracle consist of moving and being still, standing and sitting, that is not a miracle nor evidence of his truthfulness since another creature can do that. Miracles consist of things like splitting the sea, splitting the moon and other such things which a human being cannot do.

– It must break normal patterns. If someone comes at night and his sign is that the night will come after the day or the sun rise in the east in the morning, that is not a miracle because it is something which only Allah can do and it was not done for his sake. It was like that before he made his claim and like that when he made his claim. A claim of proof of Prophethood is like any other claim. If the evidence exists, it provides proof of truthfulness. Evidence is provided in the form of things which break normal patterns like turning a staff into a snake, the rock splitting and the she-camel emerging, or water springing from fingers like a spring, or similar matters which break normal patterns and can only be done by the Creator of the heavens and the earth. These signs are equivalent to a statement by the Lord informing us that what the Messenger says is the truth.

An example of this would be if there were a group of people in the presence of a king and one of the men, who was both seen and heard by the king, said, 'People! the King commands you to do this and that. The evidence for that is that the King will affirm me by one of his actions: removing his signet-ring from his hand with the intention of verifying what I say.' When the king hears his words and his claim and then does that action which attests to his truthfulness, that is equivalent to him making a statement about the truthfulness of his claim. That is the case when Allah does something which only He can do and breaks normal patterns at the hand of the Messenger: that is equivalent to His words attesting to the truthfulness of His Messenger.

– It must be claimed to testify to the Message. If the claimant says, 'My Sign is that Allah will turn this water into oil or move the earth when I tell it to shake,' then if Allah does this, it is achieved.

– It must occur in order to support this claim against those who challenge him such as when he says, 'I am a Prophet and my sign is that this she-camel will speak or that my hand will speak.' If it then speaks and says, 'He lied. He is not a Prophet,' the words that Allah created indicate that the claimant lied because what Allah did was not in keeping with his claim. This is similar to what was related from Musaylimah the Liar who claimed to be a Prophet when he spat into a well to make its water abundant and the well collapsed and all its water departed. What Allah did was a sign which negated his claim.

– It must be that no one successfully comes up with the like of what he is challenged to do. If this precondition is met, the miracle indicates the Prophethood of the one at whose hands it appears. If Allah were to bring someone who did the like of what he did when challenged to do so, that would negate his Prophethood and it would no longer be a miracle or prove his truthfulness. That is why the Almighty says, '*Let them produce a discourse like if they are telling the truth*' (52:34) and '*Or do they say, "He has invented it"? Say: "Then produce ten invented sūrahs like this."*' (11:13) It is as if He were saying, 'If you claim that Muḥammad ﷺ wrote the Qur'an and produced it, then produce ten *sūrah*s like it. If you are all unable to do so, then know that it is not something that he produced.'

It is not said that miracles with the five preconditions are limited to the truthful, because the Dajjāl, as our Prophet ﷺ said, will have immense matters appear at his hands. The difference is that one claims to be a Messenger and the other to be a Lord, and there is a great difference between the blind and the seeing. It is entirely logical for some of creation to be sent to others. This is not impossible and so it is also not unlikely for Allah to provide proofs of the truthfulness of someone who brings Divine Law and religion.

Section

If you affirm this, know that there are two types of miracle. The first is that which is famous and whose time ended at the death of the Prophet ﷺ, and the second are those transmitted by multiple traditions as being sound and confirmed and hence must be known. The precondition is that many people transmitted it and have knowledge of what they transmit and the whole chain is reliable so that it is impossible that there be any falsehood in it. This is the case with the Qur'an and the existence of the Prophet ﷺ since the Community has transmitted the Qur'an from generation to generation going back to the Prophet ﷺ whose existence is necessarily known and whose truthfulness was confirmed by miraculous proofs. The Messenger ﷺ took it via Jibrīl from his Lord. The Qur'an has been transmitted from two Messengers who are protected from adding to it or subtracting from it, and then it has been transmitted to us by such large numbers of people that it is not possible that they lie in what they transmit and hear. That is why we necessarily know that they speak the truth in what they transmit about the existence of Muḥammad ﷺ and the Qur'an arriving through him and the challenge issued by it. In respect of worldly knowledge, that is like a man's knowledge of what has been transmitted to him about the existence of places like Basra, Syria, Iraq, Khorasan, Madīnah, Makkah and similar widely known and transmitted reports.

The Qur'an will remain a miracle until the Day of Rising whereas the miracles of other Prophets ended with their death. The Qur'an will not be changed or altered as happened with the Torah and Gospel.

There are ten aspects to the inimitability of the Qur'an.

– Its wondrous composition differs from every usual order in Arabic and other languages because its arrangement is not any kind of poetry, as Allah says, '*We did not teach him poetry nor would it be right for him.*' (36:68) In *Ṣaḥīḥ Muslim*, it is reported that Unays, the brother of Abū Dharr, told Abū Dharr, 'In Makkah I met a man who claims that Allah sent him.' He asked, 'What do people say about him?' He replied, 'They say: he is a poet, a soothsayer and a sorcerer.' Unays was a poet and said, 'I have heard the words of the soothsayers and this is not like their words. I compared him with the reciters of poetry and it was not like them. No one after me should err and say he was a poet. He is truthful and they are liars.' When 'Utbah ibn Rabī'ah, known for his esteemed position in judging rhetoric and eloquence, heard the Qur'an, he affirmed that it was not sorcery or poetry and that he had never heard anything like it.

– Its style differs from all the other styles of the Arabs.

– It has a lucid, eloquent style which could not possibly come from a creature. Reflect on that in Sūrat Qāf (50), Sūrat az-Zumar (39) and Ibrāhīm (14) and you will clearly see its eloquence which a creature could not possibly originate. Ibn al-Ḥaṣṣār said, 'Anyone who knows that Allah Almighty is the Truth knows that this purity of style is not found in any other discourse.'

Ibn al-Ḥaṣṣār went on, 'These three – arrangement, purity of style and lucid eloquence – are found in every *sūrah*, indeed, in every *āyah*, and the combination of these three distinguishes the diction of every *āyah* and every *sūrah* from the words of ordinary humans. By this there is a challenge [to opponents] and inimitability. Every *sūrah* has these three, although other aspects of the ten may be ascribed to it as well. Sūrat al-Kawthar (108) consists of only three short *āyah*s, being the shortest *sūrah* in the Qur'an, and it contains reports about the unseen matters: about Kawthar and its immensity and abundance which indicates that the Prophet ﷺ will have the greatest number of Followers. The second is about al-Walīd ibn al-Mughīrah, who was a wealthy man with many children when this was revealed (74:11), and then later he was destroyed.

– The Arabic usage used in it is beyond what any Arab could master and they all agree that it is correct, with every word and letter in its proper place.

– It talks of matters which occurred from the beginning of the world until the time of its revelations, all this issuing from the mouth of someone illiterate who could neither read nor write. It reports about the stories of Prophets with their communities and past generations as well as those matters the People of the Book asked about when they challenged him about the People of the Cave, al-Khiḍr and Mūsā, and Dhū 'l-Qarnayn. Qāḍī ibn aṭ-Ṭayyib points out that we know that there was no way for him to learn this because he did not have contact with people with knowledge of history, or frequent a teacher, so that he could take from them, and so it is known that it could only have come by way of revelation.

– There is the fulfilment of Allah's promises which were visually perceived in all that He promised in the Qur'an. That is divided into general reports, like promising His Messenger ﷺ victory and expelling those who expelled him, and promises which have preconditions like, '*If someone trusts in Allah, He is enough for him*' (65:3), '*Whoever believes in Allah – He will guide his heart*' (64:11), '*Whoever has taqwā in Allah – He will give him a way out*' (65:2) '*If there are twenty of you who are steadfast, they will overcome two hundred.*' (8:65), and other examples.

– There are reports about unseen matters in the future which could only be known by revelation. Part of that is Allah's promise to His Prophet ﷺ that his *dīn* would overcome all other religions when He says, '*It is He Who sent His Messenger with the Guidance and the Dīn of Truth*' (48:28), as happened. When Abū Bakr sent his armies on expeditions, he would inform them of Allah's promise to make His *dīn* victorious so that they would be confident of victory and certain of success. 'Umar also did that, and the conquests continued in the east and west. Allah says, '*Allah has promised those of you who believe and do right actions that He will make them the successors in the land as He made those before them the successors.*' (24:55) He said, '*Allah has confirmed His Messenger's vision with truth: "You will enter the Masjid al-Ḥarām in safety"*' (48:27) and '*Alif Lām Mīm. The Romans have been defeated in the land nearby, but after their defeat they will themselves be victorious.*' (30:1-3) All of these are reports about unseen matters which only the Lord of all the Worlds knows or someone whom the Lord of the Worlds gives to know. This indicates that Allah informed His Messenger ﷺ about them so that it would be a proof of his truthfulness.

– There is the knowledge that the Qur'an contains, which is the basis for all people regarding the lawful and unlawful and other rulings.

– There are eloquent expressions of wisdom which do not normally issue from a human being.

– The perfect symmetry of the entire Qur'an, outward and inward without disparity or inconsistency, is a final factor. Allah says, *'If it had been from other than Allah, they would have found many inconsistencies in it.'* (4:82)

These are ten points mentioned by our scholars, and an eleventh, mentioned by an-Naẓẓām and some Qadarīs, is that the meaning of inimitability is the impossibility of opposition and being prevented from undertaking to meet the challenge. They said that the prohibition and diverting people from attempting to do that are the miracle rather than the Qur'an itself. That is because Allah directed their aspirations away from undertaking the challenge to bring a *sūrah* like it. This is false because the consensus of the community without any disagreement is that Qur'an itself is the miracle, not the diversion and prohibition, because its eloquence and lucidity are beyond normal patterns. If there had been any words like it, it would not be the case. This indicates that the prohibition and diversion are not the miracle.

They also have two different views about this diversion. One is that they were diverted from the ability to do it. If they had attempted it, they would have lacked the power to do it. The second is that they were diverted from undertaking it although it was within their power and they would have succeeded had they tried.

Ibn 'Aṭiyyah said, 'The substance of the challenge in the Qur'an has to do with its composition, the soundness of its meanings, and the continuous eloquence of its phrases. The substance of its inimitability is that Allah Almighty encompasses all things in knowledge and encompasses all words in His knowledge. By His all-encompassing knowledge, He knows which word is proper for following another and how to make clear one meaning after another. That is the case from the beginning of the Qur'an to the end of it. Human beings are subject to ignorance, forgetfulness and distraction. It is an indisputable fact that a human being is not all-encompassing.

'The composition of the Qur'an has the ultimate eloquence. This invalidates the position of those who said that the Arabs possessed the ability to bring the like of the Qur'an in ultimate eloquence, but when Muḥammad ﷺ came, they were diverted from that and unable to do it. What is sound is that producing something like the Qur'an is not within the power of a creature. The incapacity of the human becomes obvious to you when one of them who is eloquent produces a speech or ode exerting all his effort and continues to work at it for an entire year. Then someone else comes after him and exerts his own talent and makes alterations in it.

That continues to be done. But were someone to attempt to find a better word for one in the Qur'an, he would not be able to do that.'

Part of the eloquence of the Qur'an is that in a single *āyah* Allah mentions two commands, two prohibitions, two reports and two instances of good news. That is in '*We revealed to Mūsā's mother, "Suckle him and then when you fear for him cast him into the sea. Do not fear or grieve; We will return him to you and make him one of the Messengers."*' (28:7). The same is true of the beginning of Sūrat al-Mā'idah where He mentions fulfilling contracts, forbids breaking contracts, and makes things generally lawful and then after that makes one exception after another. Then He reports about His wisdom and power. That is something that only Allah can do. Allah reports about death, grief over loss, the reward and punishment of the Next Abode, the triumph of the successful and the ruin of the wrongdoers, cautions against being deluded by this world and describes it as being insignificant in relation to the Enduring Abode in '*Every self will taste death. You will be paid your wages in full on the Day of Rising. Anyone who is distanced from the Fire and admitted to the Garden has triumphed. The life of this world is just the enjoyment of delusion.*' (3:185). He also reports about the stories of the first and the last, the end of the affluent and outcome of those who were destroyed in half of an *āyah* in '*Against some We sent a sudden squall of stones; some of them were seized by the Great Blast; some We caused the earth to swallow up; and some We drowned.*' (29:40). He reported about the Ship, its sailing, the destruction of the unbelievers, the coming to rest and landing of the Ship and directing commands of subjugation to the heaven and the earth in '*He said, 'Embark in it. In the name of Allah be its voyage and its landing! … And it was said, 'Away with the people of the wrongdoers!"*' (11:41-44).

When Quraysh were unable to produce anything like it, they said that the Prophet ﷺ had fabricated it. So Allah revealed: '*Or do they say, "He has simply made it up?" No, the truth is they do not believe. Let them produce a discourse like it if they are telling the truth.*' (52:33-34) Then He revealed something that revealed their incapacity even more: '*Or do they say, "He has invented it"? Say, "Then produced ten invented sūrahs like this.*' (11:13) When they were still unable to do that, He decreased the amount to something like one of the short *sūrahs* and said, '*If you have doubts about what We have sent down to Our slave, produce another sūrah equal to it.*' (2:23) They were unable to respond and that was the end of it. So they resorted to war and obstinacy and preferred the capture of women and children. If they had been able to respond, it would have been far easier, a stronger argument, and would have had greater effect. They could not respond although they were masters of rhetoric and composition and were the source of eloquence in language.

The eloquence (*balāghah*) of the Qur'an possesses the highest levels of excellence and most elevated degrees of concision and clarity. Indeed, it exceeds the limits of excellence, to the sphere of masters and beyond. Although the Messenger of Allah ﷺ was given concise meaningful expressions, rare wisdoms, which you will see when you reflect on what he said in describing the Garden, and extreme excellence in language, that falls short of the rank of the Qur'an. The Prophet ﷺ said, 'In it is what no eye has seen, no ear has heard, and has not occurred to the heart of man.' See where that is in relation to the words of the Almighty: '*They will have there all that their hearts desire and their eyes find delight in*' (43:71) and '*No self knows the delight that is hidden away for it.*' (32:17)

This is the most balanced structure, beautiful composition, and sweet expression. Furthermore, that is expressed even in the amount of a *sūrah* or a longer *āyah*. That is because whenever the words are long, there is scope for departure and the words fall short for someone who falls short. So the argument was won against the Arabs since they were masters of eloquence and likely to answer back. Similarly in the case of 'Īsā ﷺ, the proof of the miracle was established against doctors and that of Mūsā ﷺ against the magicians. Allah gave the Prophets miracles in the field in which people were most skilled at that time so that the Prophet could defeat them. Magic had reached its peak at the time of Mūsā, medicine in the time of 'Īsā, and eloquence at the time of Muḥammad ﷺ.

Information about hadiths forged about the excellence of the *sūrahs* of the Qur'an and other matters

No attention should be paid to false hadiths and baseless reports about the excellence of the *sūrahs* of the Qur'an and other virtuous actions devised by forgers and opponents. Many people do this and their goals and aims vary. Some of them are *zindīqs*, like al-Mughīrah ibn Sa'īd al-Kūfī and Muḥammad ibn Sa'īd ash-Shāmī. They forged hadiths and used to create doubt in the hearts of people. One example is what Muḥammad ibn Sa'īd related from Anas ibn Mālik about the words of the Prophet ﷺ, 'I am the seal of the Prophets and there will be no Prophet after me "except as Allah wishes".' He added the exception and that is heresy on his part. This is mentioned by Ibn 'Abd 'l-Barr in the *Kitāb at-Tamhīd*. The exception is interpreted to mean dreams, and Allah knows best.

Others forged hadiths to support a sect they were inviting people to join. One of the Kharijite leaders said after he repented, 'These hadiths are the *dīn*. So look to whom you take your *dīn* from. When we desired something, we made up a hadith about it.'

Another group forged hadiths about rewards, calling people to virtuous actions, as related from Abū 'Iṣmah Nūḥ ibn Maryam al-Marwazī, Muḥammad ibn 'Ukkāshah al-Kirmānī, Aḥmad ibn 'Abdullāh al-Juwaybārī and others. Abū 'Iṣmah was asked, 'Where did you get what you have from 'Ikrimah from Ibn 'Abbās about the virtue of certain *sūrahs*?' He replied, 'I saw that people were turning from the Qur'an and busying themselves with the *fiqh* of Abū Ḥanīfah and the *Military Expeditions* of Muḥammad ibn Isḥāq and so I made up this hadith about rewards.' Abū 'Amr 'Uthmān ibn aṣ-Ṣalāḥ said in the book, *'Ulūm al-ḥadīth*, 'That is the case with the long hadith reported from Ubayy ibn Ka'b from the Prophet ﷺ about the virtues of each *sūrah* of the Qur'an. Someone investigated its transmission going back until he reached someone known and a group who forged it and the track of the forgery is clear with respect to it. The commentator, al-Wāḥidī, and those who mentioned it erred in using it in their commentaries.

Some beggars who stand in markets and mosques forge hadiths with *isnāds* from the Prophet ﷺ which they have memorised. They mention these forged hadiths along with their *isnāds*. Abū Ja'far ibn Muḥammad aṭ-Ṭayālisī said, 'Aḥmad ibn Ḥanbal and Yaḥyā ibn Ma'īn prayed in the Ruṣāfah mosque and a storyteller stood before them and said, "Aḥmad ibn Ḥanbal and Yaḥyā ibn Ma'īn related to me from 'Abd ar-Razzāq from Ma'mar from Qatādah from Anas that the Messenger of Allah ﷺ said, 'If anyone says, "There is no god but Allah," a bird is created from every word whose beak is of gold and feathers of coral.'" He began a story which would cover about twenty pages. Aḥmad looked at Yaḥyā and Yaḥyā looked at Aḥmad. He asked, "Did you say this?" He said, "By Allah, I only just heard it at this moment." They remained silent until he finished his story. Then Yaḥyā asked him, "Who told you this hadith?" "Aḥmad ibn Ḥanbal and Yaḥyā ibn Ma'īn," he replied. He said, "I am Ibn Ma'īn and this is Aḥmad ibn Ḥanbal and we have never heard this as being among the hadiths of the Messenger of Allah ﷺ. This must be a lie." "You are Yaḥyā ibn Ma'īn?" he asked. "Yes," he replied. He said, "I had not heard that Yaḥyā ibn Ma'īn was a fool and I did not know it until this moment!" Yaḥyā asked, "And why do you say that I am a fool?" He replied, "It is not as if there was no Yaḥyā ibn Ma'īn and Aḥmad ibn

Ḥanbal in the world but you two! I have written from seventeen Aḥmad ibn Ḥanbals other than this." Aḥmad hid his face in his sleeve and said, "Let him go." He went as if he was mocking them.'

These groups and those who follow in their footsteps lie about the Messenger of Allah ﷺ. It is mentioned that ar-Rashīd liked pigeons and amusing himself [by racing] them. He was give some pigeons while Qāḍī Abu-l-Bakhtarī was with him. He said, 'Abū Hurayrah related that the Prophet ﷺ said, "There is only racing with that which has claws, hooves or wings."' He had inserted 'wings'. He had forged that word for ar-Rashīd. So he gave him a splendid reward. When he left, ar-Rashīd said, 'By Allah, I know that was a lie!' He ordered that the pigeons be slaughtered. He was asked, 'What was the sin of the pigeons?' He said, 'It is because they caused someone to lie about the Messenger of Allah ﷺ.' Therefore scholars abandoned his hadiths and other things that he forged and scholars did not record his hadiths at all.

If they had confined themselves to what is established in the *Ṣaḥīḥ* collections and *Musnad*s and other books made by scholars related by the imams, they would have had enough. They abandoned the warning of the Prophet ﷺ, 'Fear Allah when reporting from other than those you know. Whoever deliberately lies about me should take his seat in the Fire.' So he ﷺ warned his Community about lying, indicating that he knew that it would happen. His warning was about what is forged by the enemies of Islam and the *zindīq*s in respect of encouragement and warning and other things. Those who do the greatest harm are those who ascribed asceticism to themselves and forged hadiths about rewards that they claim for it. People accepted their forgeries and relied on them, and so they were misguided and misguided others.

What has come on the refutation of those who attack the Qur'an and oppose the text of 'Uthmān by adding to it or removing some of it

There is no disagreement in the Community among the Imams of the Sunnah that the Qur'an is the name used to designate the Words of Allah which Muḥammad ﷺ brought as a miracle, as we have said. It is preserved in the hearts, recited on the tongues, written in the copies of the Qur'an, and known by necessity in *sūrah*s and *āyah*s. It is free of any addition or increase in words and letters. There is no need for a definition to define it or number to contain it. Anyone who claims increase or decrease in it has declared the consensus false and such an action astonishes people.

We read what Allah said about what the Messenger ﷺ brought in the Qur'an, *'Say: "If both men and jinn banded together to produce the like of this Qur'an, they could never produce anything like it, even if they backed each other up."'* (17:88). That is an attempt to invalidate the Sign of the Messenger because if it had been something someone was capable of doing, it would not be a proof or a sign and therefore not a miracle.

Those who say that there is addition or decrease in the Qur'an reject the Book of Allah and what the Messenger ﷺ has brought. It is the same as someone who states that the obligatory prayers are fifty, one can marry nine women and that Allah has made it obligatory to fast extra days together with the days of Ramadan, and so forth. As all of that is refuted by consensus, so consensus about the Qur'an is more binding and necessary.

Imam Abū Bakr Muḥammad ibn al-Qāsim ibn Bashshār ibn Muḥammad al-Anbārī said, 'The people of excellence and intelligence continue to recognise the nobility of the Qur'an and its high position. This is necessitated by truth, justice and religion. They deny the statements of nullifiers and the misrepresentation of atheists, which has led in our time to grave deviation from religion and an attack on the community in an attempt to nullify the Sharī'ah, which Allah continues to support. He makes its roots firm and its branches grow and guards it against the criticisms of those who are filled with bias and injustice and against the stratagems of the people of enmity and unbelief.'

'Such people claim that the copy of the Qur'an that 'Uthmān had transcribed, and which the Companions of the Messenger of Allah ﷺ agreed was correct, is not complete since five hundred letters are missing from it. There are also claims that 'Uthmān and the Companions added to the Qur'an. They claim that 'Uthmān was not right in assigning the transcription of the Qur'an to Zayd ibn Thābit because 'Abdullāh ibn Mas'ūd and Ubayy ibn Ka'b were more entitled to do that than Zayd, on account of the fact that the Prophet ﷺ said, 'Ubayy ibn Ka'b has the greatest knowledge of recitation in my community,' and 'Whoever is happy to recite the Qur'an fresh as it was revealed should recite the reading of Ibn Umm 'Abd.' Such a person says that he can differ from the Qur'an of 'Uthman as Abū 'Amr ibn al-'Alā', Ibn Kathīr, Nāfi', Ḥamzah and al-Kisā'ī did in respect of vowelling and doubling of certain letters. These points are not actual difference from the text as we will mention when it occurs.'

Abū Bakr continued, 'This person mentioned that Ubayy ibn Ka'b recited, "*as though it had not been flourishing just the day before and Allah only destroyed it because of the sins of its people.*" This is false because 'Abdullāh recited to Mujāhid, Mujāhid recited to Ibn 'Abbās and Ibn 'Abbās recited the Qur'an to Ubayy ibn Ka'b: "*as though it had not been flourishing just the day before! In this way We make Our Signs clear...*" (10:24) In one transmission, Ubayy recited the Qur'an to the Messenger of Allah ﷺ. This *isnād* is connected to the Messenger ﷺ and transmitted by the people of justice and integrity. When someone is sound from the Messenger of Allah ﷺ, there is no hadith to dispute it. Yaḥyā ibn al-Mubārak al-Yazīdī said, 'I recited the Qur'an to Abū 'Amr ibn al-'Alā' who recited it to Mujāhid who recited it to Ibn 'Abbās, and Ibn 'Abbās recited it to Ubayy ibn Ka'b who recited it to the Prophet ﷺ. It does not contain "Allah only destroyed it because of the sins of its people." Whoever denies that Allah revealed this addition to His Prophet ﷺ is neither an unbeliever nor a sinner.'

Ubayy related from Naṣr ibn Dāwūd aṣ-Ṣāghānī from Abū 'Ubayd: 'As for what is related about letters which disagree with the codex on which there is consensus which has *isnād*s, which are particular and not general, that they transmit from Ubayy the words, "Allah only destroyed it because of the sins of its people" and from Ibn 'Abbās "there is nothing wrong in seeking bounty from your Lord in the festivals of the Hajj," and what they relate about 'Umar ibn al-Khaṭṭāb reciting, "not of those with anger on them, nor [adding an extra *ghayr*] of the misguided" as well as many other examples, the people of knowledge do not transmit that the prayer is valid with them nor that they oppose the codex of 'Uthmān because if anyone denies that these letters are part of the Qur'an, he is not an unbeliever, but if anyone denies any part of the Qur'an collected by 'Uthmān with the agreement of the Companions, then he is an unbeliever and his ruling is that of an apostate who is asked to repent. If he does not repent, he is executed.'

Abū 'Ubayd said, 'What 'Uthmān did in transcribing the Qur'an is still considered to be one of his great virtuous actions. Some of the people of deviation attack it in order to look for his faults. Yazīd ibn Zuray' related from 'Imrān ibn Jarīr that Abū Miljaz said, "People attacked 'Uthmān ؓ for his foolishness in collecting the Qur'an and then they read what was abrogated." Abū 'Ubayd said that Abū Miljaz believed that 'Uthmān omitted what he omitted based on knowledge, as he confirmed what he confirmed, based on knowledge.'

Abū Bakr said, 'The unbelief of the person who said this [about the codex of 'Uthmān] is indicated by His words, "*It is We Who have sent down the Reminder and We Who will preserve it*" (15:9) because Allah has preserved the Qur'an from change and alteration and from addition or decrease. When someone recites the *sūrah*, "*Ruin to the hands of Abū Lahab and ruin to him!*" (111) and says "*wa murayyatuhu*" instead of "*wa-mra'atuhu*", and "*layf*" instead of "*masad*", he has denied Allah and said that He said what He did not say and altered and changed His Book. He is laying down the path for the people of atheism who want to insert into the Qur'an what will permit Islam to be stripped away. They ascribe it to like-minded people who are trying to foist these falsehoods on them and to nullify the consensus which guards Islam on whose basis the prayers are established, *zakāt* is paid and worship attended to.

'The words of the Almighty, "*Alif-Lām-Rā'. A Book whose āyahs are perfectly constructed*" (11:1) contain evidence of the innovation of this person and his departure into unbelief because the meaning of "*whose āyahs are perfectly constructed*" prevents creatures from having the power to add to it or decrease it or to falsely ascribe anything to it.'

Seeking Refuge with Allah from Shayṭān

Allah orders people to seek refuge at the beginning of every recitation when He says, '*Whenever you recite the Qur'an, seek refuge with Allah from the cursed Shayṭān.*' (16:98) This command is a recommendation, according to the position of the majority, for every time of recitation other than the prayer. There is disagreement where the prayer is concerned. An-Naqqāsh reported from 'Aṭā' that seeking refuge is mandatory in it. Ibn Sīrīn, Ibrahim an-Nakha'ī and some other people sought refuge in the prayer in every *rak'ah* and treated the command of Allah to seek refuge as applying in every case. Abū Ḥanīfah and ash-Shāfi'ī sought refuge in the first *rak'ah* of the prayer and considered all the recitation during the prayer to constitute a single act of recitation. Mālik did not think that there was any need to seek refuge in the obligatory prayers but thought it should be done in night prayers in Ramadan.

Scholars agree that the formula of seeking refuge is not part of the Qur'an nor an *āyah* of it. It is the words of the reciter, '*A'ūdhu bi-llāhi mina-sh-shayṭāni-r-rajīm* (I seek refuge with Allah from the Accursed Shayṭān).' This formula is that on which the majority of scholars agree because it concurs with the expression in the Book of Allah. It is related that Ibn Mas'ūd said, 'I say, "I seek refuge with Allah, the All-Hearing, All-Knowing from the accursed Shayṭān."' The Prophet ﷺ said to him, 'Ibn Umm 'Abd, I seek refuge with Allah from the accursed Shayṭān as Jibrīl read it to me from the Preserved Tablet from the Pen.'

Abū Dāwūd and Ibn Mājah related in their *Sunan* collections that Jubayr ibn Muṭ'im saw the Messenger of Allah ﷺ praying. ('Amr said, 'I do not know which prayer it was.') He said, 'Allah is very much greater. Allah is very much greater (three times). Praise be to Allah Abundantly. Praise be to Allah Abundantly (three times) Glory be to Allah morning and evening (three times). I seek refuge with Allah from Shayṭān and his blowing, spitting and spurring.' Spurring is madness, spitting is poetry and blowing is pride. Ibn Mājah said that madness is insanity, spitting is when a man expels air through his mouth without spittle, and pride is haughtiness.

Abū Dāwūd also related that Abū Sa'īd al-Khudrī said that when the Messenger of Allah ﷺ rose at night, he would say the *takbīr* and then say, 'Glory be to You, O Allah, and by Your praise. Blessed is Your Name and exalted are You. There is no god but You.' Then he said, 'There is no god but Allah' three times, 'Allah is very great' three times, and 'I seek refuge with Allah, the All-Hearing, all-Knowing from the Accursed Shayṭān from his spurring, blowing and spitting.' Then he would recite.

Sulaymān ibn Sālim related from Ibn al-Qāsim that the seeking refuge formula is: 'I seek refuge with Allah, the Immense from the Accursed Shayṭān. Allah is the All-Hearing, All-Knowing. *In the Name of Allah, the All-Merciful, Most Merciful.*' Ibn 'Aṭiyyah stated, 'Those who recite often change the attribute of the Name of Allah and that of the other, as when one says "I seek refuge with Allah the Glorious from the rebellious Shayṭān," and the like. I do not say that this is a good innovation nor that it is not permitted.'

Al-Mahdawī said, 'The reciters agree about reciting the seeking refuge formula at the beginning of the Fātiḥah except for Ḥamzah who does it silently. As-Suddī related that the people of Madīnah used to begin recitation with the *basmalah.* As-Samarqandī related from some of the commentators that seeking refuge is an obligation. When the reciter forgets it and then remembers at some point in his recitation, he stops and seeks refuge and then begins from the beginning again. One of them said that he seeks refuge and then returns to where he stopped. The first is the position of the authorities of the Hijaz and Iraq and the second is that of the authorities of Syria and Egypt.'

Az-Zahrawī said, 'The *āyah* was revealed about the prayer, and it was recommended to seek refuge outside the prayer, but it is not an obligation.' Another said, 'It was an obligation only for the Prophet ﷺ and we emulate him.'

If it is asked, 'What is the benefit of seeking refuge from the Accursed Shayṭān at the time of recitation?' the reply is that the benefit lies in obeying the command. The only benefit of prescribed matters lies in obeying them if they are commands or avoiding them if they are prohibitions. It is said that its benefit is to obey the command to seek refuge from the whispering of Shayṭān in recitation as Allah says, '*We did not send any Messenger or any Prophet before you without Shayṭān insinuating something into his recitation while he was reciting.*' (22:50).

Ibn al-'Arabī said, 'Very strange is what we find of the words of Mālik in the *Collection* (*Majmū'ah*) regarding the commentary on this *āyah*, "*Whenever you recite the Qur'an, seek refuge with Allah from the cursed Shayṭān*" (16:98) when he says, "That is after the recitation of the Umm al-Qur'ān for the one who recites in the prayer." This position has no effect and investigation does not support it. If it is as some people say about seeking refuge being after the recitation, it specifies that that comes after the Fātiḥah in the prayer. That is a tremendous claim and does not resemble the basic principle or understanding of Mālik. Allah best knows the secret of this transmission.'

Regarding the excellence of seeking refuge, Muslim related that Sulaymān ibn Ṣurad said, 'Two men were quarrelling in the presence of the Prophet ﷺ. One of them became angry and his face turned red and his veins stood out. The Prophet ﷺ looked at him and said, "I know a statement which, if you say it, will remove what you feel: 'I seek refuge with Allah from the accursed Shayṭān.'" A man who had heard the Prophet ﷺ went to the man and said, "Do you know what the Messenger of Allah ﷺ said? He said, 'I know a statement which, if you say it, will remove what you feel: "I seek refuge with Allah from the accursed Shayṭān."'" The man said to him, "Do you think I am mad?"' Al-Bukhārī transmitted it.

Muslim reported that 'Uthman ibn Abi-l-'Āṣ said, 'I went to the Prophet ﷺ and said, "Messenger of Allah, Shayṭān comes between me and my prayer and recitation and confuses me." He said, "That is a Shayṭān called Khinzab. When you feel that, seek refuge in Allah from him and spit to your left three times." I did that and Allah removed it from me.'

Abū Dāwūd reported that Ibn 'Umar said, 'When the Messenger of Allah ﷺ travelled, and night was coming he said, "O earth, my Lord and your Lord is Allah. I seek refuge with Allah from your evil and the evil of what He creates in you, from the evil of what crawls on you, from the lion and the black scorpion, from snakes and scorpions and the dwellers of the land, and a parent and what he begets."'

Khawlah bint Ḥakīm reported that she heard the Messenger of Allah ﷺ say, 'If anyone makes camp and then says, "I seek refuge with the complete words of Allah from the evil of what He created," he will not be harmed by anything until he sets out again.' The *Muwaṭṭā'*, Muslim and at-Tirmidhī transmitted it. He said that it is a sound *ḥasan gharīb* hadith. Seeking refuge is found and confirmed in many reports. Allah is the One Who is asked for help.

The seeking refuge formula (*isti'ādhah*) in Arabic is seeking protection in something so that it will guard a person against what he dislikes. The terms *'awdhāh, mu'ādhah* and *ta'wīdh* have the same meaning.

Shayṭān is the singular of *shayāṭīn*. The name 'Shayṭān' comes from a root (*shaṭana*) which means to be far from good. *Shaṭūn* is a deep well. *Shaṭan* is a long rope. It is called that because its ends are from far from one another. The Arabs describe a refractory horse as a shayṭān. Shayṭān himself is called that because he is far from the truth and is rebellious; and the word is used for every rebellious one among the jinn and animals. It is said that 'Shayṭān' is derived from the verb *shāṭa* which is a word used for someone who is destroyed or burned. *Ar-rajīm* (accursed) means to be far from good and humiliated. Its root means 'stoning'. 'Stoning' is a metaphor for killing, cursing, exile and abuse. All of this is found in the words of the Almighty: '*They said, "Nūḥ, if you do not desist, you will be stoned*"' (26:116) and the words of Ibrāhīm's father: '*If you do not stop, I will stone you.*' (19:46)

Al-A'mash related from Abū Wā'il from 'Abdullāh that 'Alī ibn Abī Ṭālib said, 'I saw the Messenger of Allah ﷺ at Ṣafā, facing an individual in the form of an elephant whom he was cursing. I asked, "Who are you cursing, Messenger of Allah?" He replied, "This is the accursed Shayṭān." I said, "Enemy of Allah, by Allah, I will kill you and relieve the Community of you!" He said, "This is not my repayment from you." I asked, "And what is your repayment from me, enemy of Allah?" He said, "By Allah, no one will hate you at all unless I had a share of him with his father in his mother's womb."'

The *Basmalah*

(In the Name of Allah, the All-Merciful, the Most Merciful)

Scholars say that '*By the Name of Allah, the All-Merciful, Most Merciful!*' is an oath from our Lord, which He revealed at the beginning of every *sūrah*. By it, He swears to His slaves, 'What I have laid down for you, My slaves, in this *sūrah* is true. I will fulfil for you all that I guarantee in this *sūrah* of My promise, kindness and gentleness.' '*In the Name of Allah, the All-Merciful, Most Merciful*' is part of what Allah revealed in His Book, and this is special for this Community after Sulaymān. Some scholars say that '*In the Name of Allah, the All-Merciful, Most Merciful*' contains all the Sharī'ah because it indicates the Essence and the Attributes. This is sound.

Sa'īd ibn Abī Sakīnah said that he heard that 'Alī ibn Abī Ṭālib looked at a man who was writing '*In the Name of Allah, the All-Merciful, Most Merciful,*' and told him, 'Do it well. If a man does it well, he will be forgiven.' Sa'īd said, 'I heard that a man looked at a parchment on which was written "*In the Name of Allah, the All-Merciful, Most Merciful,*" and kissed it and placed it on his eyes and was forgiven on account of that.' There is a similar story from Bishr al-Ḥāfī. When he picked up a rag on which was 'the Name of Allah' and perfumed it, his own name became honoured. Al-Qushayrī mentioned that.

An-Nasā'ī reports from Abu-l-Malīḥ about a man who rode behind the Messenger of Allah that he mentioned that the Messenger of Allah ﷺ said, 'When your animal stumbles with you, do not say, "Shayṭān has made it stumble!" because that puffs him up him until he becomes like a house and says with strength, "I have done it." Rather say, "*In the Name of Allah, the All-Merciful, Most Merciful*" and Shayṭān will become small until he is no bigger than a fly.'

'Alī ibn al-Ḥasan said about the words of the Almighty, '*When you mention your Lord alone in the Qur'an, they turn their backs in flight*' (17:46): 'That refers to when you say, "*In the Name of Allah, the All-Merciful, Most Merciful.*"' Wakī' reported from al-A'mash from Abū Wā'il that 'Abdullāh ibn Mas'ūd said, 'Whoever wants Allah to rescue him from the nineteen Zabāniyyah should recite, "*In the Name of Allah, the All-Merciful, Most Merciful*" so that Allah will make each letter a shield for him against one of them. The *basmalah* contains nineteen letters which is the same as the number of the angels of the Fire who Allah says are also nineteen. (74:30) They say in all that they do, "*In the Name of Allah, the All-Merciful, Most Merciful.* That is their strength and they take their strength from the name of Allah.'

Ibn 'Aṭiyyah said, 'The same as this is said about the Night of the Decree being the 27th night, taking note of the position the word "*hiya*" in the words of the *sūrah*, al-Qadr (97:1-5). [It is the twenty-seventh word in the *sūrah*.] And also what they say about the number of angels who hastened to report the words of the one who said, "My Lord, praise is

Yours, abundant, excellent and blessed," [after rising from *rukū'* when the Prophet ﷺ said, 'Allah hears the one who praises Him.'] It is about thirty letters. That is why the Prophet ﷺ said, "I saw about thirty angels racing to see which would be the first to write it down.'" Ibn 'Aṭiyyah added, 'This is an elegant *tafsīr*, but not a firm *tafsīr*.'

Ash-Sha'bī and al-A'mash reported that the Messenger of Allah ﷺ used to write, 'In Your Name, O Allah' until he was commanded to write 'In the Name of Allah,' and then he wrote that. When it was revealed, '*Say: "Call on Allah or call on the All-Merciful"*' (17:109), he wrote, 'In the Name of Allah, the All-Merciful.' When there was revealed, '*It is from Sulaymān and says, "In the Name of Allah, the All-Merciful, Most Merciful"*' (27:30), he wrote that. In Abū Dāwūd, ash-Sha'bī, Abū Mālik, Qatādah and Thābit ibn 'Umārah said that the Prophet ﷺ did not write '*In the Name of Allah, the All-Merciful, Most Merciful*' until Sūrat an-Naml (27) was revealed.

It is reported that Ja'far aṣ-Ṣādiq said that the *basmalah* is the crown of the *sūrahs*. This indicates that it is not an *āyah* of the Fātiḥah or other *sūrahs*. People disagree about this and have three positions regarding it.

– It is not an *āyah* of the Fātiḥah or any other *sūrah*. This is the position of Mālik.

– It is an *āyah* of every *sūrah*, and this is the position of 'Abdullāh ibn al-Mubārak.

– Ash-Shāfi'ī said that it is an *āyah* of the Fātiḥah and what he says about the other *sūrahs* varies. Sometimes he says that it is an *āyah* of every *sūrah* and sometimes that it is only one of the Fātiḥah. There is no disagreement that it is an *āyah* of the Qur'an inside Sūrat an-Naml.

Ash-Shāfi'ī's evidence is what ad-Dāraquṭnī related from Abū Bakr al-Ḥanafī from 'Abd al-Ḥamīd ibn Ja'far from Nūḥ ibn Abī Bilāl from Sa'īd ibn Abī Sa'īd al-Maqburī from Abū Hurayrah that the Prophet ﷺ said, 'When you read "*Praise belongs to Allah, the Lord of all the worlds*," then first recite "*In the Name of Allah, the All-Merciful, Most Merciful*". It is the Mother of the Qur'an, the Mother of the Book, and the Seven Mathānī. "*In the Name of Allah, the All-Merciful, Most Merciful*" is one of its *āyahs*.'

The evidence of Ibn al-Mubārak and one of the positions of ash-Shāfi'ī is what Muslim reports from Anas: 'One day while the Messenger of Allah ﷺ was among us he nodded off and then he raised his head smiling. We asked, "What has made you smile, Messenger of Allah?" He replied, "A *sūrah* was just revealed to me. It is: '*In the Name of Allah, the All-Merciful, Most Merciful. Truly We have given you the Great Abundance. So pray to your Lord and sacrifice. It is the one who hates you who is cut off without an heir.*'" (108)'

The sound position is that of Mālik because the Qur'an is not established by single reports, but by way of definitive multiple transmission about which there is no disagreement. Ibn al-'Arabī said, 'It is enough for you that there is no disagreement between people about the Qur'an. There is no disagreement about the Qur'an.' Sound reports which cannot be attacked indicate that the *basmalah* is not an *āyah* of al-Fātiḥah or any other *sūrah* except for Sūrat an-Naml. Muslim reported that Abū Hurayrah said, 'I heard the Messenger of Allah ﷺ say, "Allah says, 'I have divided the prayer into two halves between Me and My slave, and My slave will have what he asks for.' When My slave says, '*Praise be to Allah, the Lord of all the worlds*,' Allah says, 'My slave has praised Me.' He says, '*the All-Merciful, the Most Merciful*,' and the Lord says, 'My slave has lauded Me.' My slave says, '*the King of the Day of Judgement*,' and Allah says, 'My slave has magnified Me (or entrusted to Me).' The slave says, '*You alone we worship. You alone we ask for help*,' and Allah says, 'This is between Me and My slave and My slave will have what He asks for.' The slave says, '*Guide us on the Straight Path, the Path of those whom You have blessed, not of those with anger on them, nor of the misguided*,' and Allah says, 'Those are for My slave and My slave will have what He asks for.'"'

Allah said, 'I have divided the prayer', meaning the Fātiḥah, and he called it 'prayer' because the prayer is not valid except with it. So He designated the first three *āyah*s for Himself, singling them out for Himself, and the Muslims do not disagree about that. Then he made the fourth between Him and His slave because it contains the abasement of the slave and seeking help from Him. That contains esteem for Allah. Then three *āyah*s conclude the seven. They are definitely three, because He uses the plural, not the dual in 'Those are for My slave,' So '*those You have blessed*' is an *āyah*. Ibn Bukayr reported that Mālik said that '*those You have blessed*' is an *āyah*.

This is confirmed by the division and by what the Prophet ﷺ said to Ubayy when he asked Ubayy, 'How do you recite when you begin the prayer?' He replied, 'I recited, "*Praise be to Allah, the Lord of all the worlds*" to the end.' The *basmalah* was not part of it. That was the position of the people of Madīnah, the people of Syria and the people of Basra. Most reciters counted '*those You have blessed*' as an *āyah*. This is also related from Abū Naḍrah from Abū Hurayrah who said that the sixth *āyah* is '*those You have blessed*'. The people of Kufa count the *basmalah* as part of it and do not count '*those You have blessed*'.

If it is said that it is confirmed in the copies of the Qur'an that the *basmalah* is written and transmitted, as it is transmitted in an-Naml, and that this is multiple transmission, we reply that that is sound, but is it is because it is Qur'an, or is it a divider between *sūrah*s as is related from the Companions, 'We did not know the end of the *sūrah* until "*In the Name of Allah, the All-Merciful, Most Merciful*' was revealed."' (Abū Dāwūd)? Or it may be for the blessing, in the same way that the Community agrees to write it at the beginning of books and letters. All of that is possible. Al-Jurayrī said, 'Al-Ḥasan was asked about "*In the Name of Allah, the All-Merciful, Most Merciful*" and said "At the beginning of letters."' He also said, '"*In the Name of Allah, the All-Merciful, Most Merciful*" was not revealed in any of the Qur'an except an-Naml.' The criterion is that the Qur'an is not established by logic and deduction. It is established by definitive multiple transmission. So the statement of ash-Shāfi'ī about the *basmalah* being at that beginning of each *sūrah* is unsound because the *basmalah* is not an *āyah* of each *sūrah.* Praise belongs to Allah.

It is reported that a group related that the *basmalah*s are part of the Qur'an. Ad-Dāraquṭnī dealt with all of that. We do not deny the transmission of that and we have indicated it, but we have firm reports which counter it which are related by reliable imams and *fuqahā'*. In *Ṣaḥīḥ Muslim* 'Ā'ishah is reported as saying, 'The Messenger of Allah ﷺ used to begin the prayer with the *takbīr* and the recitation of "*Praise be to Allah, the Lord of all the worlds.*"' Muslim also reported that Anas ibn Mālik said, 'I prayed behind the Prophet ﷺ, Abū Bakr and 'Umar, and they began with "*Praise be to Allah.*" They did not mention "*In the Name of Allah, the All-Merciful, Most Merciful*", either at the beginning or the end of recitation.'

So our school prefers that, and it is logical. That is because the Mosque of the Prophet ﷺ in Madīnah passed through many years from the time of the Messenger of Allah ﷺ, until the time of Mālik and during all that time, following the Sunnah, no one recited, '*In the Name of Allah, the All-Merciful, Most Merciful*'. This refutes the hadiths you cite. Our people, however, prefer to recite it in the voluntary prayers, and there are traditions (*āthār*) about reciting it or an allowance for doing that. Mālik said, 'There is no harm in reciting it in the *nāfilah* or when simply reading the Qur'an.'

A group of the school of Mālik and his people said that it is not part of the Fātiḥah or any other *sūrah,* and it is not recited by the one who prays the obligatory or any other prayer, either silently or aloud. It is permitted to recite it in *nāfilah* prayers. This is well-known in his school and with his people. There is another transmission that it is recited at the beginning of the *sūrah* in *nāfilah* prayers but not at the beginning of the Fātiḥah. It is related that Ibn Nāfi' began his recitation with it in the obligatory and *nāfilah* prayers and did not ever omit it. Some of the people of Madīnah say that there must be '*In the Name of Allah, the All-Merciful, Most Merciful*,' among them Ibn 'Umar and Ibn Shihāb. Ash-Shāfi'ī, Aḥmad, Isḥāq, Abū Thawr and Abū 'Ubayd said that. That indicates that it is a matter of *ijtihād* and not definitive, as some ignorant individuals claim.

Another group of scholars believe that it is recited silently with the Fātiḥah. They include Abū Ḥanīfah and ath-Thawrī. That is related from 'Umar, 'Alī, Ibn Mas'ūd, 'Ammār and Ibn az-Zubayr. It is also the view of al-Ḥakam and Ḥammād, and it is stated by Aḥmad ibn Ḥanbal and Abū 'Ubayd. Something similar to that is related from al-Awzā'ī. The evidence for that is the report from Anas ibn Mālik: 'The Messenger of Allah ﷺ led us in the prayer and we did not hear him recite, "*In the Name of Allah, the All-Merciful, Most Merciful*."'

This is a good position, and the traditions (*āthār*) reported from Anas agree on it and remove the disagreement about the recitation of the *basmalah*. It is related that Sa'īd ibn Jubayr said, 'The idolaters used to come to the mosque. When the Messenger of Allah ﷺ recited, "*In the Name of Allah, the All-Merciful, Most Merciful*," they said, "This Muḥammad mentioned the Raḥmān of Yamāmah," meaning Musaylimah. So he was commanded to recite it silently and it was revealed, "*Do not be too loud in your prayer or too quiet in it.*" (17:110)' At-Tirmidhī al-Ḥakīm said, 'That has lasted until now, even if the cause no longer exists, as running remains in *ṭawāf* even if the cause no longer exists and silence in the day prayers even if the cause no longer exists.'

The Community agree that it is permitted to write it at the beginning of every book of knowledge and letter. If it is a volume of poetry, Mujālid related that ash-Sha'bī said, 'The consensus is that they do not write "*In the Name of Allah, the All-Merciful, Most Merciful*" before poetry.' Az-Zuhrī said, 'The sunnah is not to write "*In the Name of Allah, the All-Merciful, Most Merciful*" in poetry.' Sa'īd ibn Jubayr believed that it is written in the front of books of poetry and many later scholars corroborate that. Abū Bakr al-Khaṭīb said, 'That is our choice and what we prefer.'

Al-Māwardī said that someone who says, '*bismi-llāh*' is called a '*mubasmil*'. The term is used in poetry. What is famous in language is [to use the verb] *basmala*. Ya'qūb ibn as-Sakīt, al-Muṭawwir, ath-Tha'ālabī and others said that *basmala* is the verb for someone saying '*bismi-llāh*' or when he says it often.

The Sharī'ah recommends mentioning the *basmalah* at the beginning of every action, like eating, drinking, slaughtering, sexual intercourse, purification, embarking on a ship and the like. Allah says, *'Eat that over which the name of Allah has been mentioned'* (6:119) and He said, *'Embark in it. In the name of Allah be its voyage and its landing!'* (11:41) The Prophet ﷺ said, 'Lock your door and mention the Name of Allah. Put out your lamp and mention the Name of Allah. Cover your vessel and mention the Name of Allah. Tie up your water-skin and mention the Name of Allah.' He said, 'If anyone of you wants to go to his wife, he should say, "In the Name of Allah. O Allah, keep Shayṭān away from us and keep Shayṭān away from what You provide us with." If a child is decreed for them, Shayṭān will not harm him at all.' He told 'Umar ibn Abī Salamah, 'Boy, say the name of Allah Almighty and eat with your right hand and eat what is in front of you.' He said, 'Shayṭān considers food lawful when the Name of Allah is not mentioned over it.' He said, 'Whoever has not slaughtered should slaughter in the Name of Allah.'

When 'Uthmān ibn Abi-l-'Āṣ complained to him of a pain he had in his body since he had become Muslim, the Messenger of Allah ﷺ said to him, 'Place your hand on that part of your body which pains you and say "In the Name of Allah" three times and then say seven times, "I seek refuge in the might and power of Allah from the evil of what I feel and am on my guard against."' All of this is confirmed in the Ṣaḥīḥ. Ibn Mājah and at-Tirmidhī report that the Prophet ﷺ said, 'The veil between the jinn and the private parts of the sons of Ādam when he enters the privy is to say, "In the Name of Allah."' Ad-Dāraquṭnī reported that 'Ā'ishah said, 'When the Prophet ﷺ touched his *wuḍū'* vessel, he said the Name of Allah and then poured the water on his hands.' Our scholars say that this refutes the Qadarites and others who say that our actions are decreed by them. The argument against them in that is that Allah commanded us to begin every action with the *basmalah.*

The meaning of 'In the Name of Allah' is 'by Allah', and the meaning of 'by Allah' is by His creating and decreeing one reaches whatever one reaches. Some say that 'In the Name of Allah' means 'I begin with the help, success and blessing of Allah.' This is Allah teaching His slaves to mention His Name at the beginning of recitation and other actions so that one begins with the blessing of Allah.

There is disagreement about the meaning of adding *'ism'* ('the name of'). Quṭrub said that it is added to increase the esteem and respect of mentioning Allah Almighty. Al-Akhfash said that it is added to remove it from the possibility of being an oath to being a prayer for blessing, since the root is '*bi-llāh*'. They also disagree about the meaning of adding the *bā'* ('in', 'with'). Does it have the meaning of a command so that it implies: 'Begin with the Name of Allah.' Or is it a report which implies: 'I have begun with the Name of Allah." Al-Farrā' takes the first view and az-Zajjāj takes the second. In both views it is in the accusative case. It is said that it means: 'My beginning is in the Name of Allah.' '*Bismillāh*' is written without the *alif* of '*ism*' as there is no need of it when the *bā'* is connected to the written word because it is a frequent usage.

There is disagreement about the derivation of *ism* (name), with two basic positions. The Basrans say that it is derived from *sumuw*, which means height and elevation. It is said that *ism* means that the person is in an elevated place. It is said that the name lifts the named above others. It is said that the name is called that because it is higher than the other parts of speech by its strength. The noun (*ism*) is stronger by agreement because it is the root. These are three statements.

The Kufans say that it is derived from *simah*, which means a sign, because the Name is a sign of the One to whom it is given. So the root of *ism* is *wasam*. The first is sounder because of the form of the diminutive (*sumayy*) and the form of the plural which is *asmā'*. Another disagreement indicates the soundness of that, and it is the next point.

If it is true that *ism* is derived from height, Allah was described by it before creation existed, after it existed and will be when it is annihilated, and creatures have no effect on the Names or Attributes. This is the position of the people of the Sunnah. Those who say that it is derived from *simah* say that before time Allah was without name or attribute. When He created creatures, they gave Him Names and Attributes. When He annihilates them, He will again have no name or attribute. This is the position of the Mu'tazilites, and it is contrary to that on which the Community agree. It is worse than their error when they say, 'His Word is created.' Exalted above that is Allah! It is according to this that there is a disagreement about the Name and Named.

The people of truth believe, as Qāḍī Abū Bakr ibn aṭ-Ṭayyib al-Bāqillānī mentioned, that the name is the thing named and Ibn Fūrak is content with that. It is the position of Abū 'Abīdah and Sībawayh. If someone says 'Allah is Knowing', his words indicate the Essence, which is described as being knowing. So the Name is Knowing and it is what is Named. It is the same when someone says, 'Allah is the Creator.' The Creator is the Lord and it is the Name itself. So their view is that the

Name is the Named itself with no distinction.

Ibn Ḥaṣṣār said, 'Those among the innovators who deny the attributes claim that namings have no meaning except the Essence. That is why they say that the Name is not the Named. Whoever affirms the Attributes, affirms that the names have meanings which are qualities of the Essence. They are not expressions, but they are Names in their view.' More of this will come in al-Baqarah and al-A'rāf.

Allah is the greatest and most comprehensive of all the Names, so that one scholar said that it is the Greatest Name of Allah and no one else has it. That is why it has no dual or plural. That is one of two interpretations of the words of the Almighty, *'Do you know of any other with His Name?'* (19:65), in other words, is there anyone named with His Name which is Allah? Allah is the Name of the True Existent who has all the Divine Attributes and is described as Lord and alone possesses real existence. There is no god but Him. Glory be to Him! It is said that it means the One who alone is worthy of worship. It is said that it means the One whose existence is necessary who always was and always will be. The meaning is the same.

There is disagreement about whether this Name is etymologically derived or a unique designation for the Divine Essence. Many of the people of knowledge believe the first but then disagree on its actual derivation and root. Sībawayh reported from al-Khalīl that its root is *ilāh*, on the measure of *fi'āl*. The *alif* and *lām* replace the *hamzah*. Sībawayh said that it is like *an-nās* (people) whose root is *unās*. It is said that its root is *lāh* and the *alif* and *lām* are added to exalt it. This is what Sībawayh preferred. Al-Kisā'ī and al-Farrā' said that '*bismillāh*' is made up of '*bismi – al-ilāh*' and elision has occurred and the first *lām* assimilated into the second and so becomes a double *lām*.

It is said that the name Allah is derived from *walaha*, to be bewildered. *Walah* means loss of intellect, and someone who is *wālih* is bewildered. Allah bewilders minds when they think on the realities of His attributes and reflect on gnosis of Him. So the basis of this *ilāh* is *walāh* and the *hamzah* is changed from the *wāw*. That is also reported from al-Khalīl. It is related that aḍ-Ḍaḥḥāk said, 'Allah is called a God because creatures devote (*ta'allaha*) themselves to Him in their needs and make supplication to Him in times of hardship.' It is related that al-Khalīl ibn Aḥmad said something similar. It is also said that it is derived from elevation and that the Arabs used to use *lāh* for something elevated and they used the verb (*lāhat*) for sunrise.

It is said that the name Allah is derived from the word *ilāh* (god), which means what a man worships as He says, '*abandon you and your gods (ālihataka).*' (7:127) They said that it means 'your worship'. They said that the name 'Allāh' is derived from this and so the meaning of 'Allah' is the Object of Worship. So what the unifiers say, 'There is no god but Allah' means 'there is no object of worship other than Allah.' Here '*illā*' means 'other than (*ghayr*)', not 'except.' Some claim that the root is the *hā'* which alludes to the third person. That is since they affirm Him as existing in their natural intellects and indicate Him with the letter of allusion. Then the *lām* of possession is added to it since they know that He is the Creator and Master of things, and *al* then is added for magnification.

The second position is taken by a group of scholars, including ash-Shāfi'ī, Abu-l-Ma'ālī, al-Khaṭṭābī, al-Ghazālī, al-Mufaḍḍal and others, and is related from al-Khalīl and Sībawayh. It is that the *alif* and *lām* are a necessary part of it and cannot be elided from it. Al-Khaṭṭābī said that the evidence that the *alif* and *lām* are an intrinsic part of the structure of this name and not added as the definite article is that it is included in the vocative, as 'Yā Allāh!' The vocative is not combined with the definite article *alif-lām*. One does not say, 'Yā ar-Raḥmān'. [but rather Yā Raḥmān]. Allah knows best.

There is also disagreement about the derivation of ar-Raḥmān. Some of them said that it has no derivation because it is one of the names particular to Him, and if it had been derived from mercy (*raḥmah*), it would be connected to the one shown mercy and it would be possible to say, 'Allah is Raḥmān to His slaves,' as one does with *raḥīm*. If it had been derived from *raḥmah*, the Arabs would not have denied it when they heard it because they did not deny the mercy of their Lord. Allah says, '*When they are told to prostrate to the All-Merciful, they say, "And what is the All-Merciful?"* (25:60)'

At al-Ḥudaybīyah, when 'Alī wrote at the command of the Prophet ﷺ '*In the Name of Allah, the All-Merciful, Most Merciful,*' Suhayl ibn 'Amr said, 'As for the words "*In the Name of Allah, the All-Merciful, Most Merciful,*" we do not know "*In the Name of Allah, the All-Merciful, Most Merciful*"! Rather write "In Your Name, O Allah."' Ibn al-'Arabī says that this indicates that they did not know the attribute rather than the One Described. Evidence is found in the fact that they said, '*What is the Raḥmān?*' not 'Who is the Raḥmān?' Ibn al-Ḥaṣṣār said, 'It is as if he, may Allah be merciful to him, had not recited the other *āyah*, "*Yet they still reject the All-Merciful.*" (13:31)' The majority of people believe that it is derived from *raḥmah*, and is intensive, meaning the One who possesses mercy such as no one else has. It has no plural or dual whereas *raḥīm* can be dual or plural.

Ibn al-Ḥaṣṣār said that part of what indicates the derivation is what at-Tirmidhī transmitted as sound from 'Abd ar-Raḥmān ibn 'Awf. He heard the Messenger of Allah ﷺ say, 'Allah Almighty says, "I am the All-Merciful. I created kinship (*raḥim*) and split it as a name from My Name. Whoever maintains ties, I maintain ties with him. Whoever severs it, I sever him."' This is a text indicating its derivation and so there is no point in contention about it. The denial of the Arabs was simply due to their ignorance of Allah and what is mandatory for Him.

Al-Anbārī mentions in *az-Zāhir* that al-Mubarrad stated that ar-Raḥmān is a Hebrew name. Abū Isḥāq az-Zajjāj says in *Ma'ānī al-Qur'ān* that Aḥmad ibn Yaḥyā said that ar-Raḥīm is Arabic and ar-Raḥmān is Hebrew. This view is unwarranted.

Abu-l-'Abbās says that the attribute is for praise as you might say, 'Jarīr the poet.' Muṭarrif related that Qatādah said that '*In the Name of Allah, the All-Merciful, Most Merciful*' is Allah praising Himself. Abū Isḥāq says that this is a good position. Quṭrub says that it is possible that the two are combined for stress. Abū Isḥāq says that this is also a good position and using it for stress has a greater benefit and that is often used in Arabic. There is no need to attest to it. The benefit in that is what Muḥammad ibn Yazīd said: 'It is favour after favour and blessing after blessing, and it strengthens the hopes of those who desire and is a promise which will not fail.'

There is disagreement about whether the two names Raḥmān and Raḥīm have one meaning or two meanings. It is said that they mean the same, as do *nadmān* and *nadīm*. It is said that Raḥmān is a special name with general action and Raḥīm is a general name with a particular action. This is the position of the majority.

Abū 'Alī al-Fārisī said that Raḥmān is a general name for all types of mercy for which Allah is singled out. Raḥīm can be used for how He is towards the believers, as He says, '*He is merciful (Raḥīm) to the believers.*' (33:43). Al-'Arazamī says that Raḥmān is merciful to all His creatures with rain, physical and general blessings, and Raḥīm is merciful to the believers in guiding them and being kind to them. Ibn al-Mubārak said that when the Raḥmān is asked He gives and when the Raḥīm is not asked, He is angry. Ibn Mājah related in the *Sunan* and at-Tirmidhī in *al-Jāmi'* from Abū Ṣāliḥ from Abū Hurayrah that the Messenger of Allah ﷺ said, 'If someone does not ask, Allah is angry with him.' At-Tirmidhī transmitted it. The version in Ibn Mājah has: 'If someone does not make supplication to Allah, He is angry with Him.' Ibn Mājah said, 'I asked Abū Zur'ah about this Abū Ṣāliḥ. He said, "This is the one who is called al-Fārisī. He is Khūzī. I do not know his name."' One of the poets took this idea and said:

Allah is angry when people fail to ask of Him
while the sons of Ādam are angry when they are asked.

Ibn 'Abbās said that they are two fine (*raqīq*) names, and one is finer than the other, meaning that it has more mercy. Al-Khaṭṭābī said, 'This is problematic because fineness has no place in any of the attributes of Allah.' Al-Ḥusayn ibn al-Faḍl al-Bajalī said, 'This is an error on the part of the transmitter because fineness (*riqqah*) is not part of the attributes of Allah at all. Rather they are two compassionate (*rafīq*) names, one more compassionate than the other. Compassion is one of the Attributes of Allah Almighty. The Prophet ﷺ said, "Allah is Compassionate. He loves compassion and gives for compassion what He does not for harshness."'

Most scholars agree that the name ar-Raḥmān is used only for Allah Almighty and it is not permitted to call anyone else by it. Do you not see that He says: '*Say: "Call on Allah or call on the All-Merciful"*' (17:109)? So it is equal to the Name in which none but Him shares. He says: '*Ask those We sent before you as Our Messengers: Have We ever designated any gods to be worshipped besides the All-Merciful?*' (43:44) So they reported that the Raḥmān deserved worship. Musaylimah the Liar – may Allah curse him – was outrageous and called himself 'the raḥmān of Yamāmah' and so was called 'the Liar'. It is the term by which he was known. It is also said that the name ar-Raḥmān is the Greatest Name of Allah. Ibn al-'Arabī mentioned that.

Ar-Raḥīm is general and can be used in respect of creatures. As ar-Raḥmān is universal, so it is brought forward in order before ar-Raḥīm in harmony with revelation. Al-Mahdawī stated that. It is said that the meaning of ar-Raḥīm is: 'It is by the Raḥīm that you reach to the Raḥmān.' So ar-Raḥīm is the attribute of Muḥammad ﷺ and Allah described him as having that quality; He says: 'compassionate, merciful (*raḥīm*)' when describing him. So it as if the meaning of saying, '*In the Name of Allah, the All-Merciful, the Most Merciful*' is 'It is by Muḥammad ﷺ that you will reach Me,' in other words, 'by following him and what he has brought, you will reach My reward, honour and the vision of My face.' Allah knows best.

It is related that 'Alī ibn Abī Ṭālib said, '*Bismillāh* is healing from every illness and protection against every disease. Ar-Raḥmān is a help for everyone who believes in Him. It is a name not used for anyone else. Ar-Raḥīm is for those who repent, believe and perform righteous actions.'

Some of them explained the meaning according to the letters. It is related that 'Uthmān ibn 'Affān ※ asked the Messenger of Allah ※ about the interpretation of '*In the Name of Allah, the All-Merciful, the Most Merciful.*' He said, 'The *bā'* is the trial (*balā'*) of Allah, His relief, brilliance and radiance (*bahā'*). The *sīn* is the splendour (*sanā'*) of Allah. The *mīm* is the kingdom (*mulk*) of Allah. As for Allah, there is no god but Him. The Raḥmān is kind to both the pious and impious of His creatures. The Raḥīm is kind only to the believers.' It is reported that Ka'b al-Aḥbār said, 'The *bā'* is His radiance (*bahā'*), the *sīn* is His splendour (*sanā'*), and there is nothing higher than it. The *mīm* is His kingdom, and He has power over all things and nothing is hard for Him.'

It is said that every letter is the opening of one of His Names. The *bā'* is the key to His Name *Baṣīr* (All-Seeing). The *sīn* is the key to His Name, *Samī'* (All-Hearing). The *mīm* is the key to His Name, *Mālik* (Master). The *alif* is the key to His Name, Allah. The *lām* is the key to His Name, *Laṭīf* (Kind). The *hā'* is the key to His Name, *Hādī* (Guide). The *rā'* is the key to His Name, *Rāziq* (Provider). The *ḥā'* is the key to His Name, *Ḥalīm* (Forbearing). The *nūn* is the key of His Name, *Nūr* (Light). The meaning of all this is supplication of Allah at the beginning of everything you do.

There is disagreement about how 'ar-Raḥīm' is connected in recitation to 'al-ḥamdu lillāh'. Umm Salamah related that the Prophet ※ recited 'ar-Raḥīm' with a *sukūn* on the *mīm*, stopping there and then beginning with a fresh *alif*. Some of the Kufans recited it in that way. Most people recite, 'ar-Raḥīmi-l-ḥamdu', with a *kasrah* on the *mīm* and connecting it to the *alif* in *al-ḥamd*. Al-Kisā'ī reported that some Arabs read it 'ar-Raḥīma-l-ḥamdu', with *fatḥah* on the *mīm* and connected to the *alif*, as if the *mīm* was in fact silent, but with an elision into the *alif*. Ibn 'Aṭiyyah said, 'This recitation is not reported from anyone I know.'

www.ingramcontent.com/pod-product-compliance
Lightning Source LLC
LaVergne TN
LVHW061346060426
835512LV00012B/2579
9781908892577